THE ART OF
SCREENWRITING

The Art of Screenwriting

STORY · SCRIPT · MARKETS

William Packard

THUNDER'S MOUTH PRESS
New York

THE ART OF SCREENWRITING

Copyright © 1987, 1997 by William Packard

Published by
Thunder's Mouth Press
An Imprint of Avalon Publishing Group Incorporated
161 William St., 16th Floor
New York, NY 10038

Library of Congress Cataloging-in-Publication Data

Packard, William.
The art of screenwriting.

Bibliography:
Includes index.
1. Moving-picture authorship. I. Title.
PN1996.P23   1986   808.2'3 86-22517
ISBN 1-56025-141-7
This edition ISBN 1-56025-322-3

9 8 7 6 5 4 3 2 1

Printed in the United States of America
Distributed by Publishers Group West

This book is dedicated to
OTTO PREMINGER
with gratitude for his encouragement
and enduring example.

CONTENTS

CONTENTS

Foreword

THE ART OF FILM

Imagine a young person somewhere out in Kansas—halfway between New York and Los Angeles, the twin meccas of filmmaking in America.

A young person—he or she (we'll use the masculine pronoun through the rest of this book for the sake of simplicity, so long as it is clearly understood that filmmaking today is as open to women as it is to men). So, imagine that this young person is out walking through an open field under a high wide sky, somewhere there in Kansas. And suddenly, wonderfully, an extraordinary thing begins to happen—in something approaching a rapture or an ecstasy, this young person begins telling himself a story that might make for an overwhelmingly powerful motion picture. And as he tells himself the story, he begins to see the whole scenario unfold right there in front of him, and it is all there—real characters with strong actions which are expressed in sharp clear visuals, and the whole thing is developed along the spine of a thrilling cinematic story line.

Who knows, this young person might be imagining

something as stark and vivid and exciting as one of the great classic films, like *Potemkin* or *All Quiet on the Western Front* or *Citizen Kane*. Or else he might be imagining something as timely and vibrant and alive as one of the modern film masterpieces like *The Grapes of Wrath* or *Psycho* or *On the Waterfront*.

Does this sound too fantastic? But films are made of just such fantasies, out of our most highly imaginative moments, when we are overcome by the genius of some unknown energy that comes and moves through us to create something far greater than we ever thought we could create.

But any film, no matter how great, has to begin somewhere—even in the imagination of a young person walking through an open field under a high wide sky, somewhere there in Kansas.

Or else, to put it another way—film itself, all film, the experience of film, had to begin somewhere. And it did begin, a very long time ago, with man's earliest awareness, and with his deep need to tell a story, and his endless fascination with the illusion of movement which seems to recreate the action of life itself.

Once upon a time there were toys that seemed to make images move—drawings on rotary discs that danced or jumped when the discs were spun, and paddle wheels that made objects shift position rapidly, and riffle books one could flip through and see moving figures making jerky movements. And all these devices were using a technique known as persistence of vision, which is the same principle that enables separate film frames to create an illusion of movement in motion pictures.

Then there was the actual development of film —photography using silver nitrate which turns dark when light strikes it, to create a negative effect. The first photograph was taken around 1816, and Louis DaGuerre invented the daguerrotype in 1837, which Oliver Wendell Holmes called "the mirror with a memory."

Not long after, the first motion picture projectors were

designed around 1845, and by 1875 a man with the oddly spelled name of Eadweard Muybridge was using multiple shutters on a single plate camera to create more than one image at a time. And when Leland Stanford made a wager that all four feet of a trotting horse were off the ground at the same time, Eadweard Muybridge went to Stanford's farm in Palo Alto, California, and set up 24 cameras along a raceway to capture sequential shots of a horse in motion. This was the first use of time lapse photography and it proved that Stanford was right, all four feet of the horse were in fact in the air at the same instant.

The modern camera was invented by W. K. L. Dickson, and Thomas A. Edison shot the first movie on a film base produced by George Eastman in 1889. But while Eastman is generally credited with the invention of motion pictures, he didn't seem to take the whole idea very seriously, and he was content to show film through a Kinetoscope with the viewer's eyes looking down through a slot at the top. Edison was never much interested in projecting these images onto an external screen, nor did he even bother to take out a European patent on his invention because, as he said, "It's not worth it."

Even so, by 1893, the Edison Company had built a studio in West Orange, New Jersey, where there was one fixed camera using sunlight. Fred Ott, an actor, did a prolonged sneeze on Edison's camera, and this became the first extended motion picture in history. Others also experimented—Dickson was making films of Buffalo Bill and Annie Oakley, and Eadweard Muybridge began exhibiting his movies at the Chicago World's Fair where one reporter described his motion pictures as "a magic lantern run mad."

In 1894, Woodville Latham perfected a machine that was similar to Edison's Kinetoscope, only this one projected the moving images onto an outside screen. By 1896, the American Biograph Company produced a film, *The Empire*

State Express, and in Europe, Georges Méliès was showing motion pictures at Théâtre Robert-Houdin. And in 1899, the first fight film was made, using indoor lighting, of the Jeffries-Sharkey match.

In 1903, Edwin Porter produced the revolutionary film, *The Great Train Robbery,* which told a continuous story for the first time and included scenes on top of a speeding train with bandits fighting for control of the steam engine. In 1907, there was a film version of *Romeo and Juliet,* and in 1908 a one-reel film titled *The Lonely Villa* was made by a young director named D. W. Griffith which had the first use of intercutting scenes of parallel action. In 1909, there was the first animated cartoon, *Gertie the Dinosaur.*

This era of these early silent films was an augury of the immense power and scope that films would come to have for the rest of the century. Some people still tried to deny the importance of films—Edison himself called them "this champion time-waster." And D. H. Lawrence was openly contemptuous of the new film medium:

> Since that triumph of the deaf and dumb, the cinematograph, has come to give us the nervous excitment of speed—grimace, agitations, and speed, as of flying atoms, chaos—many an old church in Italy has taken a new lease on life.[1]

But others were not so scornful of film and foresaw the enormous power that movies would exercise in our lives. Rudolph Arnheim, writing in *Film as Art,* describes this early era as an adventure analogous to the heroic ocean-going explorers, before filmmaking became a mere middle class diversion:

> Film is a unique experiment in the visual arts which took place in the first three decades of this century. In its pure state it survives in the private efforts of a few courageous individuals; and occasional flares, reminis-

cent of a distinguished past, light up the mass production of the film industry, which permitted the new medium to become a comfortable technique for popular story-telling.[2]

More than mere story-telling, film was also a pioneer art that would have profound implications on international affairs, domestic politics, economics, anthropology, sociology, military strategy, and even the nascent science of psychoanalysis. Sigmund Freud published *The Interpretation of Dreams* in 1900, basing his revolutionary theory of the unconscious on classical myth and great Greek plays like the *Oedipus Rex* by Sophocles. One wonders how differently Freud would have shaped his theory if he had had motion pictures to draw on for illustration—the work, say, of master filmmakers like Ingmar Bergman, Bernardo Bertolucci, John Ford, Alfred Hitchock, and Akira Kurosawa. As it was, Freud did not see his first film until 1909, while he was in New York City on his way to Clark University in Worcester, Massachusetts—he sat and watched an early silent movie and was "quietly amused" at the sight of "a lot of wild chasing." That might have been an end to it, but Ernest Jones reports that later, in 1925, Samuel Goldwyn approached Freud with the preposterous offer of $100,000 if Freud would collaborate in making a film with scenes from all the famous love stories of history, beginning with *Antony and Cleopatra*. Again, Freud was quietly amused, but with characteristic integrity he refused the offer outright and would not even see the American film mogul. Even so, films were quick to pick up on the implications of Freud's new psychoanalytic insight—not only in such direct treatments as *Lady in the Dark* in 1944, and *Psycho* in 1960, and the film biography of *Freud* in 1962, but also in a whole host of films which indirectly assume Freud's principal teachings of the unconscious—dream interpretation, infantile sexuality, and the Oedipal complex.

Others also saw film as an opening up of colossal proportions. In 1915, the American poet Vachel Lindsay wrote one of the earliest books of film criticism, a solid work entitled *The Art of the Moving Picture*, and in it he proclaimed Thomas Edison as "the new Gutenberg. He has invented the new printing." And in Europe, Lenin was among the first to hail the tremendous power and scope of films when he said, "The most important of all the arts is cinema." And Adolf Hitler foresaw the enormous potential of film for propaganda purposes, when he commissioned Leni Riefenstahl to make a motion picture of the 1936 Olympics, a spectacularly photographed epic film titled *The Triumph of Will*. And to this day movies exercise an extraordinary power to influence international affairs—most American films are automatically banned from the Soviet Union, and Stanley Kubrick's 1957 film *Paths of Glory* is banned in France because it tells the true story of how three French soldiers in World War One were chosen by lot and executed when their company failed to achieve an impossible military objective. And in the United States, a great deal of the credit for ending the Vietnam War has to go to the cameramen who filmed the awful napalm horrors of that conflict so Americans could see for themselves, right there on their home television screens, what a senseless war they were perpetrating.

And, if film has a great potential to influence politics and social thought, it has an even greater potential to agitate a community in the arena of public morals. In 1896, a film titled *The Widow Jones* showed a man and woman in an extended kiss, and this first cinematic intimacy triggered outcries of indecency among early audiences. With time, a strict moral censorship was rigidly imposed on film subject matter by the early Hays Code and the Catholic Legion of Decency and the Motion Picture Producers Association. Things were so carefully repressed that in 1936, the first film version of Lillian Hellman's *The Children's Hour*, entitled *These Three*, had to alter its subject matter from suspected lesbianism to suspected adultery (as if that made it any more virtuous!). To his great credit, the film's director, William Wyler, went on to make a second film version of *The Children's Hour* in 1961 with Audrey Hepburn and Shirley MacLaine, which restored the subject matter to its original theme of suspected lesbianism. And even as late as 1953, Otto Preminger's film *The Moon is Blue* caused a furor because it dared to use the word "virgin" on the sound track, and in 1955 Preminger was denied a Seal of Approval from the Motion Picture Producers Association for his film *The Man with the Golden Arm* because it dared to deal openly with drug addiction. And when Stanley Kubrick made *Lolita* in 1962 from Vladimir Nabokov's frisky novel about an erotic nymphet, because of prevailing morēs he could not depict the obsessive titillation of the horny romp as graphically as he felt he had to—so the film version tends to be more heady and intellectual than the novel is.

Not only films, but also the off-screen lives of those who are actively engaged in filmmaking have tended to agitate the community conscience to an inordinate degree. In some cases, off-screen sex scandals have seriously impeded the careers of some of our greatest film artists, from Charlie Chaplin and Fatty Arbuckle to Ingrid Bergman. And this insistence on a veneer of virtue became so prevalent that during the 1920s and 1930s, most of the major film studios had so-called "morality clauses" written right into their actors' contracts. In other cases, off-screen political opinions were just as much of an obstruction to the careers of many great film artists, as witness Paul Robeson and the persons named on the infamous Hollywood Black Lists. We may flatter ourselves that we are beyond such barbaric piety today, but a good deal of the hypocrisy lingers in the air aound us so that the ongoing notoriety of a distinguished screen actress like Elizabeth Taylor periodically obscures her real achivement as a consistently excellent film artist. In fact, there is such an appetite for gossip and scandal associated with anything that takes place in Hollywood, sometimes it takes someone as strong and straightforward as Marlon Brando to tell off the press: "I have no right to ask *you* personal questions. Why, because I'm an actor, have you the right to ask me?"

Even so, for better or worse, motion pictures have

become a history of our time, and today we more or less take film for granted as the most popular and influential medium of the twentieth century. We have film departments in our leading schools and universities which offer B.F.A. and M.F.A. programs in film studies, and most municipal museums and libraries have film archives for early classic, documentary and historical films.

And to assuage our perennial concern for community morals, we have adopted a voluntary rating system for commercial films—"G" for general, "PG" for parental guidance, "R" for restricted, and "X" for red hot material—to guide us in our choice of films within the limit of what we think our moral sensibilities can safely tolerate. There is even the cryptic "PG-13," wherein "Parents Are Strongly Cautioned to Give Special Guidance for Attendance of Children Under 13—Some Material May Be Inappropriate for Young Children"—which reads like the Surgeon-General's wordy warning on a pack of cigarettes, and probably has about as much effect.

Indeed, film has become such a large part of our lives that sometimes we are afraid that movies may become a poor substitute for life itself. And it is true that movies can be an escape for the empty and a soporific for the mindless and an opiate for the distressed, and some poor lost souls have come to live so vicariously through the films they see that they do not have any real lives of their own. Nowhere is this situation expressed more eloquently than in *The Glass Menagerie* of Tennessee Williams, when Tom says:

> People go to the movies instead of moving! Hollywood characters are supposed to have all the adventures for everybody in America . . . I'm tired of the movies and I am about to move![3]

But, regardless of whether we think films are as revolutionary as the Gutenberg printing press, or nothing but a champion time-waster, there can be little doubt that movies today have emerged as the most commercial art commodity of our time. And there is also a good case to be made for film as the most complete medium that has ever been conceived by the mind of man, and the chief testament and record of our pathetic adventures here on this planet earth.

Nevertheless. Our initial question still remains—what about that young person who is out walking through an open field under a high wide sky, somewhere in Kansas? How can this young person hope to break into the film industry with his original cinematic story line? How should he go about trying to translate his creative ideas into an effective screenplay treatment? And then how should he package this treatment and get an agent to market his property? And once it has been sold, how should the screenwriter begin to set down his story line in the appropriate full-length finished screenplay format? And what should a screenwriter know about how to protect his work during the various stages of film production? Because during the actual shooting of his film, will the young screenwriter be able to face the fact that in most cases he is simply there to make the raw clay which will then be handed over to others for further play and shaping? Will he be able to stay sane through all the radical cuts and outrageous changes and left field interpolations that may take place, before his original story line is ready to reach the silver screen?

This book tries to answer all these technical, legal, business and psychological questions which are the nuts and bolts of the screenwriting profession. And the book also attempts to answer the much larger artistic questions—what is the art of film itself, and how should the screenwriter relate to that great collaborative process which takes place in the film industry?

Because the peculiar thing about filmmaking is that it is simultaneously both a business and an art form, and the screenwriter must be aware of his dual function in scripting a movie. He must be both an artisan and an artist —responsible both to his employer for the product he was hired to execute, and also responsible to his conscience for maintaining the integrity of his own work.

This dual function of the screenwriter is often confused in the film industry itself, and when that happens the screenwriter can suffer untold agonies over the absurdities that are perpetrated on his original screenplay in the name of some inane "development" or "improvement" or "realization." He may often have to stand aside helplessly and watch as everyone from the makeup man and the lighting technician to the script-girl begin to exercise an input on what was originally the screenwriter's own cinematic story line—that thrilling creative idea that first came to him, in something approaching a rapture or an ecstasy, perhaps when he was out walking through an open field under a high wide sky, somewhere there in Kansas.

And at times like this, a screenwriter may feel so betrayed, so depressed, and so bereft of any instinct to go on, that he may end up cursing the very screenwriting profession he was trying his damnedest to represent.

But occasionally, with breaks in the game or the grace of the gods, the two screenwriting functions of artisan and artist may happily coincide, and the screenwriter may accidentally find himself on the same wave length with the producer and the director and the actors and the cameraman, and everyone is working harmoniously together towards one common goal. And when this happens, it will feel as if everyone is catching magic from each other's imagination, and any changes that may be made will be gladly welcomed by all the persons at work on the film, including the screenwriter, because everyone will realize that he is part of a much larger artistic process.

And at times like this, a screenwriter may feel authentic joy to be involved in such an exalted creative enterprise, and he will even feel enormous pride to be a representative of the screenwriting profession.

PREFACE

William Packard is playwright, a screen writer, and a poet. He understands from first-hand experience the problems and joys of each medium and has written a fascinating and highly informative book which should become required reading not only for students but for all professional artists of stage and screen, and for all technicians working in these arenas.

I was very fortunate to appear in his adaptation of Racine's Phèdre in New York and London, produced by that fine organization, IASTA. This was an exceptional experience for me as an actress since he understands so well the actor's world as well as that of the writer.

I am sure that the experience of reading this book will prove to be valuable as preparation and help for the problems that a screen writer must face, not only at the typewriter, but on the way to the front office and beyond. The knowledge gained will surely build the confidence that is needed to suceed in the world of shadow and light.

Beatrice Straight

Beatrice Straight's distinguished career on stage and in film has earned her a Tony Award for her performance in Arthur Miller's play The Crucible, *and an Academy Award for her performance in the film* Network. *Her interpretation of the role of Phèdre, in William Packard's translation of the Racine play, earned her the Outer Circle Critics Award.*

xix

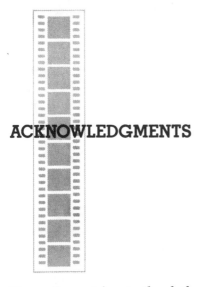

ACKNOWLEDGMENTS

The author wishes to thank the following persons who gave so generously of their time and understanding, in private conversations and interviews, to help make this book on the art of screenwriting:

To screenwriting agents Bret Adams and Mary Harden of THE BRET ADAMS AGENCY; to Rosanne Ehrlich, Literary Director of PARAMOUNT PICTURES; to union representatives Jim Kaye and Mona Mangan of THE WRITERS GUILD OF AMERICA/EAST; to poet Leo Connellan for his comments on the creative process; to Michael Manzi of the Dramatic Writing Program at New York University; to actors Jose Ferrer and Joan Fontaine and Michael Moriarty for their invaluable lifetime experience; to screenwriter Venable Herndon for his friendly help on every phase of this book and for permission to reprint his film treatment and pages from his screenplay with Arthur Penn of ALICE'S RESTAURANT; to Joe Wang of PRAGAN CAMERA for his recommendations on basic camera equipment; to Jon Imparato for his advice on foreign films; to Shelly Estrin for her advice on the great portraiture and landscape painters; to Herbert Berghof of the H. B. STUDIO for his devotion to the living principles of the art.

One

WHERE DID SCREENWRITERS COME FROM?

Most of us are not so sure what filmmaking is all about.

We like to go and see films, and we sit and watch as the credits are listed in the opening titles—there are the names of the star actors, and then there are the names of the producer and the director, and there are all those other names—the editor, the cameraman, the art director, the costume director, the sound technician, the make-up artist, the musical director. And then towards the end, there is the name of the screenwriter.

And then we sit back and watch the film itself, although in the back of our minds we are not sure what all those names of all those people mean, and we do not understand very much about the different things they are supposed to be doing. And if we think about it, sometimes we get even more confused if we try to figure out who does what, exactly, in the making of a film.

And we get even more confused every time we watch the Oscar ceremonies on television. Every year The Academy of

Motion Picture Arts and Sciences gives its annual awards to a whole host of categories of filmmaking. In the beginning (1927/1928), there were only a modest 12 awards for outstanding achievement:

BEST PRODUCTION	WRITING *(adaptation)*
BEST ACTOR	WRITING *(title)*
BEST ACTRESS	CINEMATOGRAPHY
BEST DIRECTION	ART DIRECTION
BEST DIRECTION *(comedy)*	ENGINEERING EFFECTS
WRITING *(original story)*	ARTISTIC QUALITY OF PRODUCTION

Now, almost 60 years later, there is a total of over 25 categories, as if the previous award list had been broken down into more and more specific detail descriptions:

BEST PICTURE	ART DIRECTION *(color)*
BEST ACTOR	COSTUME DESIGN *(black and white)*
BEST ACTRESS	
BEST SUPPORTING ACTOR	COSTUME DESIGN *(color)*
BEST SUPPORTING ACTRESS	SOUND
BEST DIRECTION	SOUND EFFECTS
BEST FOREIGN LANGUAGE Film	FILM EDITING
	SPECIAL EFFECTS
WRITING *(screenplay based on material from another medium)*	MUSIC *(score—substantially original)*
WRITING *(best story and screenplay written directly for the screen)*	MUSIC *(scoring—adaptation or treatment)*
	MUSIC *(song)*
CINEMATOGRAPHY *(black and white)*	SHORT SUBJECTS *(cartoon)*
	SHORT SUBJECTS *(live action)*
CINEMATOGRAPHY *(color)*	DOCUMENTARY *(short subject)*
ART DIRECTION *(black and white)*	DOCUMENTARY *(feature length)*

If we compare these two Academy Award lists, we can see how the film industry itself has grown in sophistication and specialization as the art form passed through an era of unsurpassed expertise and technology. From the crude beginning of movies—1927 was the same year the first sound film, *The Jazz Singer* with Al Jolson, was produced —motion pictures have explored every innovation one could possibly imagine. From the sweeping expanse of wide screen cinemascope to 3-D horror films where bats seem to fly right off the screen and into the screaming audience, movies have achieved the most extraordinary visual effects imaginable. There has been synchronized animation as in *That's Entertainment* in 1974, a review of all the great MGM musicals where Gene Kelly seems to be dancing with a couple of cartoon characters: there has been trick photography as in *Lady in the Lake* in 1946 where Robert Montgomery walks through an entire film seeming to see everything from his own character's point of view; and there has been miniaturization as in the opening scene of *Henry V* in 1945, where the entire city of London is recreated in small-scale detail, complete with tiny cathedrals and infinitesimal smokestacks sending up wee wisps of blue fumes, and the Thames River is filled with a special oil-base fluid to make it seem to move slowly along the banks of the early Elizabethan city.

Films have, indeed, grown in technique and complexity, so much so that it only intensifies our confusion if we try to figure out who does what, exactly, in the making of a film.

And the area we seem to be most confused about is screenwriting. We've never been quite sure what the screenwriter's contribution is to the completed film, exactly.

Now that we think of it, we doubt if we have ever gone to see a film simply because we knew that a certain screenwriter had written it. We've gone to see films with favorite star actors, or to see favorite directors, but never to see "a favorite screenwriter"— and that strikes us as odd.

Of course, we may have gone to see certain writers, indirectly. There were all those wonderful films based on the plays of Shakespeare, beginning with the 1935 Max Reinhardt production of *A Midsummer Night's Dream;* and there were the three Olivier masterpiece films of *Henry V* (1945), *Hamlet* (1948), and *Richard III* (1955); and there was the Orson Welles film of *Macbeth* (1948); and there was the 1953 Joseph Mankiewicz film of *Julius Caesar* with Marlon Brando and John Gielgud and James Mason; and there were 13 film versions of *Romeo and Juliet,* beginning with the 1936 film with Leslie Howard and Norma Shearer and John Barrymore, all the way on up to the ravishing 1968 Zeferelli film that was shot in Verona.

And we have gone to see films because they were adaptations based on the work of some of the greatest novelists. There was Tolstoy's *Anna Karenina* filmed in 1948 with Vivien Leigh and Ralph Richardson, and *War and Peace* in 1956 with Henry Fonda, Mel Ferrer and Audrey Hepburn. And the work of Charles Dickens was filmed as *David Copperfield* in 1935 with W. C. Fields and Lionel Barrymore, and *A Tale of Two Cities* in 1936 with Ronald Coleman, and *Oliver Twist* in 1948 with Alec Guinness. And the Bronte sisters are represented on film with *Wuthering Heights* in 1939 with Laurence Olivier and Merle Oberon, and *Jane Eyre* in 1944 with Orson Welles and Joan Fontaine.

And of course we have gone to see films that were based on stage plays we may already have known—the work of Arthur Miller served to make films such as *All my Sons* (1948) and *Death of a Salesman* (1952). Tennessee Williams has probably been involved with more screenwriting of his own work, and more adaptations based on his plays, than any other American playwright—there are the two versions of *The Glass Menagerie* (1950 and 1973), *A Streetcar Named Desire* (1951), *The Rose Tattoo* (1955), *Baby Doll* (1956), *Cat on a Hot Tin Roof* (1958), *The Fugitive Kind* (1959), *Suddenly, Last Summer* (1960), *Summer and Smoke* (1961), *Sweet Bird of Youth* (1962), and *The Night of the Iguana* (1964). And there is the stage play of Edward Albee, *Who's Afraid of Virginia Woolf?*, which was made into a film in 1966 with Elizabeth Taylor, Richard Burton, Sandy Dennis and George Segal.

But aside from all these adaptations, have we ever gone to see a film simply because we knew a certain screenwriter had written an original filmscript for the movie?

Probably not. Perhaps a few of us might recognize and admire the original work of certain screenwriters, such as Budd Schulberg or Paddy Chayevsky or William Inge or Harold Pinter or Woody Allen.

And perhaps we may go to see certain foreign films like the work of Ingmar Bergman or Bernardo Bertolucci, because we admire their screenplays as much as we admire their casting of actors and their direction.

But that may be as far as most of us could go, in identifying the work of any particular screenwriter in the film industry. And as we said, that strikes us as odd.

We don't really know why this should be, in a literate civilization that prides itself on honoring the written word. And the truth is that Hollywood has, from time to time, made spectacular efforts to dignify the film industry by employing at one time or another such distinguished writers as F. Scott Fitzgerald, William Faulkner, Dashell Hammett, Tennessee Williams, Nathaniel West, Anita Loos, W. Somerset Maugham—and we can't forget that S. J. Perelman scripted a good many of the early Marx Brothers films.

In fact, Hollywood has occasionally made grandstand gestures to accommodate screenwriters as the most important single factor in the film industry. As early as 1919, before the advent of sound, Samuel Goldwyn announced that "the greatest American novelists of today" would write for his studio, with an absolute guarantee that each picture "will not be offered for release until the author has given his personal approval of it." Goldwyn boasted, "It's more difficult to find a great story than a great star." This sounded terrific, but it didn't last very long, and soon the major studios were back to their old habit of employing screenwriters to write screenplays that had been taken away from other screenwriters, and the status of screenwriter reverted to that of a hack, a lackie, and a studio employee.

5

Because the plain truth is, if we can admit that we feel confused about the role of the screenwriter in the film industry, it's because the film industry itself has always been confused about the role of the screenwriter.

All you have to do is glance at the various Academy Awards for screenwriters since their inception in 1927, and you will detect a profound confusion as to the precise role and function of screenwriting in the film industry. Notice how many different titles and designations there are for the screenwriter:

WRITING *(original story)* 1927
WRITING *(adaptation)* 1928
WRITING *(title)* 1927
WRITING *(achievement)* 1928
WRITING *(best written screenplay)* 1935
WRITING *(original screenplay)* 1940
WRITING *(motion picture story)* 1948
WRITING *(story and screenplay)* 1949
WRITING *(screenplay)* 1950
WRITING *(screenplay-adapted)* 1956
WRITING *(screenplay-original)* 1956
WRITING *(screenplay based on material from another medium)* 1957
WRITING *(story and screenplay written directly for the screen)* 1957

Those last two categories are the ones that the Academy of Motion Picture Arts and Sciences finally settled on, and today they are the bases of the Oscar awards for screenwriting. But behind all that wording there is obviously a long history of confusion over just what screenwriting itself is all about.

In fact, the very term "screenwriter" has gone through a whole host of meanings, and has signified any one of a number of functions. A screenwriter may be someone who

scripts an original screenplay property—or he may be someone who works over someone else's original screenplay
property—or he may be someone who does a lot of adaptations from plays or novels or biographies or histories—or he
may be someone who's good at making instant rewrites on
the set—or he may be someone who is a mere writer for hire,
who executes the ideas and desires of studio executives who
like to think that they're writers—or he may be someone
who is a complete underling paid on a weekly basis so he can
be fired at a moment's notice if his presence should ever
become an irritant to anyone.

The important thing to realize is that in any or all of the
above capacities, the screenwriter is always considered a
writer for hire, someone who develops a property that will
ultimately belong to somebody else.

This is such an extraordinary situation that we really
ought to explore how and why it came to be this way, and
what special circumstances have conspired to make the
screenwriter such a crazy quilt of possible duties and functions.

A lot of the circumstances have to do with the very nature
of film itself. The average two hour feature film consists of
roughly 1/3 dialogue and 2/3 visual action, and the 1/3
dialogue portion is generally assigned to the screenwriter
and the 2/3 action portion is usually left in the hands of the
director and the actors. In fact, depending on the degree of
latitude a director exercises over the film, a major part of that
1/3 dialogue portion may be left in the hands of the director
and the actors also.

Why should this be? Why shouldn't the screenwriter have
equal control over the 2/3 visual action portion of a film, and
why shouldn't he share equal billing and authority in the
making of a film, with the director and the actors?

To answer this question, we have to go back to the way
films developed in this country over this century.

There were always powerful producers, and there were
always strong directors, and there were always star actors

involved in the process of filmmaking. But there were not always screenwriters.

In fact, in the early silent films, there were no screenwriters at all. Studios like Paramount and Triangle were turning out over 100 feature films a year, and studios like Universal and Fox were racing to keep up with this pace. In addition to feature films, there were also dozens of weekly serials—two-reelers of up to 30 episodes each, which were continued on a week-to-week basis in movie theatres across the country, such as *The Perils of Pauline* with Pearl White, *The Hazards of Helen*, and Hal Roach's *Our Gang* comedies. And there were also all those *Tarzan* and *Rin-Tin-Tin* and *Andy Hardy* films, and Westerns were also a fast staple with heroes like Tom Mix and William S. Hart.

And for all these early films, there were no "screenwriters" in any realistic sense of the term. There were just a lot of idea men who took part in some pretty furious barnstorming sessions that went into the making of these motion pictures. For example, when Mack Sennett formed his famous Keystone Cops, that madcap gang of incompetents who were always into wild chases, sight gags, pratfalls and pie throwing, how did the individual films get scripted? The answer to that is simple—they didn't. There were no scripts, there were just gag conferences. And James Agee tells how Sennett hired a "wild man" to sit in on these conferences, and the wild man's entire job was to think up "wildies":

Usually he was an all but brainless, speechless man, scarcely able to communicate an idea; but he had a totally uninhibited imagination. He might say nothing for an hour; then he'd mutter, "you take . . ." and all the relatively rational others would shut up and listen.[4]

This "wild man" may sound pretty zany to us, being as Agee says, "an all but brainless, speechless man," but he goes a long way towards explaining the bemused and contemptuous and patronizing way that screenwriters will be seen later on by their colleagues. Indeed, this wild man may well be the prototype of the modern screenwriter.

Meanwhile during this early period of silent films, producers and directors and star actors began to assert total control over the film industry, and it's important for us to understand how and why these three roles came to dominate filmmaking—to the exclusion of the screenwriter.

With the growth of the Hollywood studio system came the major studio producers—giants in the field, impressarios and astute businessmen like Cecil B. DeMille, who had worked with David Belasco in New York and knew how to use stage lighting to create interesting technical effects. And men like Jesse Lasky and Samuel Goldwyn. These producers were men who epitomized everything that was excellent in silent filmmaking, and some of their early feature films show the studio system at its most spectacular and flamboyant. Movies like DeMille's epic 1923 film *The Ten Commandments*, or the 1924 *Ben Hur* with Francis X. Bushman which cost well over two million dollars—these films remain landmarks of the filmmaking art.

But while many of these top studio producers loved film, the fact is that they did not know very much about how it was put together. Otto Preminger writes in his autobiography:

In calmer retrospect, I see that much of (Sam) Goldwyn's curious behavior was due to the fact that he didn't understand the technical side of film-making. He was a showman with a great instinct, but cameras and other mechanical equipment completely baffled him.[5]

And in fact, the mentality of some of these early studio producers was so far removed from the actual process of filmmaking, that in 1919 four of the greatest film artists in the industry—Mary Pickford, Douglas Fairbanks, Charlie Chaplin, and D. W. Griffith—banded together to form their own studio, United Artists.

In addition to the studio producers, there were the star actors who also epitomized everything that was excellent in silent films. We could make our own list of some of these outstanding star actors in silent pictures:

LIONEL BARRYMORE	RUDOLPH VALENTINO
HARRY CAREY	JOHN BARRYMORE
SARAH BERNHARDT	WILL ROGERS
THEDA BARA	WALLACE BEERY
GLORIA SWANSON	LON CHANEY
JOHN GILBERT	

And there were also the top comic star actors:

BEN TURPIN	FATTY ARBUCKLE
HAROLD LLOYD	BUSTER KEATON
JOHN BUNNY	STAN LAUREL
MARIE DRESSLER	OLIVER HARDY

And of course there was one star actor who dominated American silent films—with his wide eyes and black mustache and straight cane and derby hat and baggy tramp pants. Charlie Chaplin was able to transcend the facile pranks and pratfalls of early silent film comedy by playing a naive eros who displayed courtly manners in the face of catastrophe and who finally yielded with a plaintive shrug, tipped his hat and turned and wandered away from it all. It was not so much what Chaplin did, as what he did not do—he did not recreate the rote acting style of his contemporaries who all looked like they knew they were on camera, he simply let his own inner life flow through his character so he appeared as insouciant and true as the tramp clown he was portraying. Whether he was playing a lost soul in *The Kid* with Jackie Coogan in 1920, or a sad misfit in *The Gold Rush* in 1925 who sits down to eat his own shoe, or a frantic workman in *Modern Times* in 1936 who tries to keep up with the insanity of a runaway machine age, Chaplin's genius endowed his comic character with a sense of bittersweet ludicrous pathos which showed us our own true human condition in all its agelessness. As Chaplin himself wrote:

The comedy that amuses the world today, is identically the same as that which made the inhabitants of Babylon, the Greek and Roman populace writhe and roll over with merriment in their big open-air stadiums. Only the methods have changed.[6]

And in addition to the studio producer and the star actor of silent films, there was one genius director who epitomized everything that was excellent in films—D. W. Griffith, who is credited with inventing or developing almost all of the important filmic techniques:

close-up
fade-out
iris dissolve
intercutting
back lighting
use of moving camera to follow action

Griffith was the first American director to treat film as a serious art form, and by combining his camera work with a sophisticated sense of editing, he was able to create entirely new textures of cinematic expression. Griffith directed the first so-called feature film in 1915, *The Birth of a Nation*, with Lillian Gish, which was an epic spectacle with panoramic long shots of battle scenes which had a startling realism.

So, during this period of early silent films, the studio producer and the star actor and the genius director were laying the groundwork and creating the vocabulary of film art. And still, there were no screenwriters on the scene.

Then came the revolution. In 1927, Warner Brothers produced *The Jazz Singer* with Al Jolson singing and talking onscreen through the invention of Vitaphone, a Western

Electric process, and an entirely new era began. Al Jolson spoke the prophetic first words on film:

Wait a minute . . . wait a minute . . . you aint heard nothin yet!

This sudden advent of sound in motion pictures explains the ambiguity which surrounds the role of the screenwriter in the film industry today.

Before talking pictures, D. W. Griffith directed over 500 films in five years, and Lillian Gish makes the startling comment that in the nine years that she worked with Griffith, there was never any written script at all. Griffith just gave his ideas to the actors, and then he encouraged them to develop the ideas on their own, and the cameras began filming. And of course Charlie Chaplin had worked out his own art of silent mime to such a consummate degree that there was no need for a written script.

But after 1927 and the advent of sound, there was an immediate need to save time and money in filmmaking. And so, because of the enormous expense of all those lights and the cost of the film itself with its new sound track, to say nothing of the salaries of all those extras who were standing around on the set, all the dialogue had to be set down on paper in a working filmscript before turning the camera on the actors. Everything suddenly began to get so costly, it was no longer possible to allow for as much improvisation and experiment in filmmaking as there had been during the era of silent films.

So the screenwriter was brought in fast, almost as an afterthought to the film industry. In fact, the screenwriter was brought in so fast that no one, not even the screenwriter, could figure out exactly what he should do or how he should go about doing it.

Of course none of this would have happened if Thomas Edison had cared more about his invention of moving pictures, and if he had put sound with film from the very beginning. And the irony is that Edison could very easily have made talking pictures from the outset if he had really wanted to, but he just wasn't all that interested in the future of the film medium.

So the screenwriter was born of necessity and nurtured in confusion, a late arrival in the film industry who was predestined to linger in the background as an ambiguous figure who was never entirely trusted by any of his fellow artists on the set. Or worse, the screenwriter was made into a studio hack, a yes-man whom the producers could toy with. As Joan Fontaine tells it:

> Producers wanted the writers under their thumb, they wanted them as an audience at their lunches in the Green Room. They didn't care, the writers were buyable. Anyone, including an actor, was buyable, and so wasn't of any value. And these producers had nothing but contempt for anyone they could put on salary. But they wanted them. I mean, if Shakespeare were alive today, they'd have gotten him and kicked him upstairs to an attic office once they had him . . .[7]

This contempt for writers even extended to contempt for the classics which the screenwriters were being hired to adapt for film. Joan Fontaine continues:

> These producers were illiterate and they were educating themselves—by *Vanity Fair* and *David Copperfield* and so on. They didn't know what the hell these things were, they just said it's a great big classic, and everybody knows it, so okay, let's buy it. That's what happened!

Even so, out of all this contempt and confusion and ambiguity over the role of the screenwriter in the film industry, one can only wonder at the astonishing range and scope of screenwriting that took place during the first decade of sound films. There was a wealth of imaginative and original screenwriting, and excellent adaptations from the classics, and outstanding film biographies:

1927   *Wings*
        The Way of All Flesh
        Seventh Heaven

1928   *The Bridge of San Luis Rey*

1929   *All Quiet on the Western Front*

1930   *Anna Christie*

1931   *Dr. Jekyll and Mr. Hyde*

1932   *A Farewell to Arms*
        I am a Fugitive from a Chain Gang
        The Sign of the Cross
        Frankenstein
        Tarzan, the Ape Man

1933   *The Emperor Jones*

1934   *Cleopatra*
        It Happened One Night

1935   *Lives of a Bengal Lancer*
        Mutiny on the Bounty
        A Midsummer Night's Dream
        The Last Days of Pompeii
        David Copperfield

1936   *A Tale of Two Cities*
        Romeo and Juliet
        Show Boat
        The Green Pastures
        The Story of Louis Pasteur
        Mr. Deeds Goes to Town

1937   *Lost Horizon*
        Snow White and the Seven Dwarfs
        The Life of Emile Zola
        Captains Courageous
        A Star is Born
        The Good Earth

And in the fifty years of talking films which followed that first decade of movie-making, the range and scope of screenwriting increased even more astonishingly. It would be hard to imagine an art form which could produce so many radically different styles and types of scripting.

Here is a rough rundown of the most outstanding American films over this 1938–1972 period—an inevitably subjective checklist, to be sure, but enough to show the tremendous achievement of screenwriters during the first half century of American filmmaking:

1938	*You Can't Take it with You*
	Boys Town
1939	*Of Mice and Men*
	Gone with the Wind
	Wuthering Heights
	The Wizard of Oz
1940	*The Grapes of Wrath*
	The Philadelphia Story
	Rebecca
1941	*Citizen Kane*
	How Green Was My Valley
	The Maltese Falcon
	Suspicion
	Sergeant York
1942	*Yankee Doodle Dandy*
	Casablanca
1943	*Watch on the Rhine*
	The Song of Bernadette
	For Whom the Bell Tolls
	The Human Comedy
1944	*Gaslight*
	None but the Lonely Heart
	Jane Eyre

1945 *The Lost Weekend*

1946 *The Big Sleep*
      The Best Years of Our Lives
      To Each His Own
      The Razor's Edge

1948 *The Treasure of the Sierra Madre*
      Key Largo
      All My Sons

1949 *All the King's Men*
      The Heiress

1950 *All About Eve*
      Sunset Boulevard
      Cyrano de Bergerac

1951 *An American in Paris*
      A Place in the Sun
      A Streetcar Named Desire

1952 *Singin' in the Rain*
      High Noon
      Viva Zapata!
      Death of a Salesman

1953 *Stalag 17*
      From Here to Eternity

1954 *On the Waterfront*
      The Country Girl
      Rear Window

1955 *Marty*
      Carmen Jones
      Rebel without a Cause
      The Rose Tattoo
      Mister Roberts
      East of Eden

1956 *War and Peace*
      Lust for Life

1957 *Paths of Glory*
   The Three Faces of Eve

1958 *Cat on a Hot Tin Roof*
   Vertigo

1959 *Anatomy of a Murder*
   The Fugitive Kind

1960 *Psycho*
   Sons and Lovers
   Suddenly, Last Summer

1961 *Judgment at Nuremberg*
   Summer and Smoke
   In Cold Blood
   Splendor in the Grass

1962 *Sweet Bird of Youth*
   The Miracle Worker
   Days of Wine and Roses

1963 *Long Day's Journey into Night*

1964 *The Night of the Iguana*

1965 *The Pawnbroker*

1966 *Who's Afraid of Virginia Woolf?*

1967 *Bonnie and Clyde*

1968 *2001: A Space Odyssey*
   A Lion in Winter

1969 *Butch Cassidy and the Sundance Kid*
   Bob and Carol and Ted and Alice

1970 *Joe*
   Five Easy Pieces
   Diary of a Mad Housewife

1972 *The Godfather*
   Cabaret

We can leave it to the reader to fill in the rest of the list with more recent films—perhaps including some of the following outstanding American films:

Alice's Restaurant	*The Deer Hunter*
All That Jazz	*Deliverance*
Annie Hall	*Midnight Cowboy*
Apocalypse Now	*Nashville*
Bang the Drum Slowly	*On Golden Pond*
Bound for Glory	*Ordinary People*
Chinatown	*Raging Bull*
A Clockwork Orange	*Taxi Driver*
Coalminer's Daughter	*Tender Mercies*
Coming Home	

Now we can make an interesting experiment. If we were to create a similar minimal listing of the outstanding foreign films of the last half century, we would notice a striking difference in screenwriting values. Whether because foreign films are usually under the direct supervision of one person, or because foreign films are not so yoked to a preposterous star system and studio budget considerations, these foreign films seem more seriously committed to the development of a strong original story line than American films usually are. Perhaps this is because foreign filmmakers did not inherit a sense of ambiguity and confusion concerning the screenwriter's relation to the rest of the film industry, so the problem of filmscripting can be squarely faced without a backlog of attitudes that range all the way from indifference to contempt.

Here is a list of the foreign films, and the reader can judge for himself:

ENGLAND   *Saturday Night and Sunday Morning*
Sunday, Bloody Sunday
The Entertainer
The Devils

ITALY

Rossellini—*Open City*

Fellini—*La Dolce Vita*
8 1/2
La Strada
Satyricon

Bertolucci—*Last Tango in Paris*
1900

De Sica—*Shoe Shine*
The Bicycle Thief
A Brief Vacation

Pasolini—*The Gospel According to Saint*
Matthew Salo, or the 120 Days of
Sodom

Zeferelli—*Romeo and Juliet*

Visconti—*Rocco and His Brothers*

SWEDEN

Widerberg—*Elvira Madigan*

Bergman—*The Seventh Seal*
Wild Strawberries
The Magician
Through a Glass Darkly
Persona
Cries and Whispers
Scenes from a Marriage
The Magic Flute

FRANCE

Renoir—*The Rules of the Game*
The Grand Illusion

Truffaut—*400 Blows*
Shoot the Piano Player
Jules and Jim
La Femme du Côte

Godard—*Breathless*
Weekend

Resnais—*Hiroshima, Mon Amour*
Last Year in Marienbad

POLAND	Wajda—*Ashes and Diamonds*
	Polanski—*Macbeth*
RUSSIA	Kalatozov—*The Cranes Are Flying*
	Eisenstein—*Ten Days that Shook the World*
	Potemkin
	Alexander Nevsky
	Ivan the Terrible
BRAZIL	Marcel Camus—*Black Orpheus*
JAPAN	Kurosawa—*Rashomon*
	Throne of Blood
	Ran
GERMANY	Herzog—*Aguirre, Wrath of God*
	Fassbinder—*Fear Eats the Soul*
	Beware the Holy Whore
AUSTRALIA	Beresford—*Braker Morant*

Again, this kind of listing is subjective and the reader is welcome to fill in the rest of his own choices—with films of Greece, Israel, and other countries. Then the reader can compare this listing of foreign films with our previous listing of outstanding American films to see if he agrees with our point that foreign films are more seriously committed to strong original story lines than American films are.

Whatever one thinks, the fact remains that over the present century, film in this country simply developed too fast and too expensively to allow the screenwriter to take his rightful place beside the studio producer and the genius director and the star actor.

There are other factors, also, which continue to affect the way screenwriters are seen in the American film industry.

One factor is the rapidly increasing sophistication of filmmaking techniques, which tends to propel the film art far beyond the range of ordinary screenwriting skills. For example, the use of extremely mobile and hand-held cameras has opened up the kind of shots one can take, and also modern editing techniques have made it possible to achieve intercutting effects that could not have been imagined before. Thus, in an era of ultra-high technology, the screenwriter has to try and stay alert to the changing state of his art, to be able to take full advantage of the medium in his own writing.

Another factor which continues to affect the way screenwriters are seen is the subtly changing nature of the film audience. Early silent films played to cheap seats in old vaudeville houses, and the audiences tended to be lower class patrons who were seeking immediate sensation and occasional fast laughs at the novelty of it all. By the 1940s, films began to be shown in elaborate art-deco palaces like The Roxy and Radio City Music Hall, and the audiences tended to be middle class citizens who went to the movies for romance or euphoria and to reinforce their own unconscious value systems. Today, movies are shown in unadorned film houses that are more like stark screening rooms, and the audiences tend to be representative of all classes, with a strong turnout of the young and the intellectual and the educated upper classes. And again, all a screenwriter can hope to do about this subtly changing nature of film audiences is to make himself stay aware of who is going to see what movies today, and why.

The screenwriter may still occupy a position of ambiguity and confusion within the film industry today, but he should be aware that miracles do happen. That is to say, occasionally a good screenwriter can exert a decisive influence over the making of a film. And in the long run, that can be a pretty encouraging thing because, as one of our greatest screenwriters once said,

> How films have changed!—for the better. They have outstripped the theatre in honesty, adventure, and technique, despite the fall of the big studios with their star system. Or possibly because of it?[8]

Two

WRITING FOR FILMS AS OPPOSED TO WRITING FOR THE STAGE · TIME AND SPACE ON FILM · FILM ACTING

Often you hear someone say, why don't they just film that stage play the way it is? Why do they have to go on rewriting the whole thing to make a screenplay adaptation out of it, when it already works well enough as it is up there on stage?

We can get some insight into the nature of screenwriting if we realize what an enormous difference there is between stage plays and filmscripts. Plays and films are different approaches to the same thing, just as oils and water colors are different approaches to the same thing—they may seem to be similar, but their separate natures require completely separate techniques.

And perhaps a good place for us to start is to think of how we feel when we go to see a play, and how we feel when we go to see a film. Because our own experiences with these two mediums may give us all the clues we need to figure out why and how they are so different from each other.

Going to the theatre is a public act—we usually get dressed up for the occasion and we go into a well-lit theatre and are probably aware of the people sitting around us. Then the house lights dim and the play begins. During the intermission we get up and leave our seats and go out into the lobby to stretch our legs and have a cigarette and perhaps discuss the performances. Then we go back inside to our seats and the play begins again. And when the play is all over, we applaud the actors and we leave the theatre feeling somehow moved and elated that we managed to identify with something that was taking place up there onstage.

But going to see a film is much more of a private experience—we usually don't bother getting dressed up for it and we go into a dimly-lit movie house and we are not particularly aware of the people around us, and we sit there wholly enclosed in the darkness as we watch what is happening up there on that huge screen. There is no intermission, so we are able to remain totally engrossed in our own experience. And then, when the film is over, we do not applaud—we just get up and leave the movie house. And as we step out onto the sidewalk and into the real world again, for an instant we feel a slight shock of disorientation that is not unlike jet lag.

All these clues indicate to us that seeing stage plays has something to do with our deepest beliefs, whereas seeing film has something to do with our deepest being. And now we have to figure out why and how this should be so.

To see how film can affect us in our deepest being, we need some sense of what film is, in itself, that sets it apart from stage plays or novels or any other literary and dramatic mediums. In *The Art of the Moving Picture*, published in 1915, Vachel Lindsay gives us a useful approach when he divides all films into three types:

DRAMATIC—   action films, like war stories,
                adventures and westerns

LYRIC—   intimate films, like love stories
                and stories of self-discovery

EPIC— spectacle films, like period stories and stories of costume pageantry

That's about as good a breakdown of major feature films as we could want—although we're aware that there are also a good many other types of more specialized films that can be made, for example:

DOCUMENTARY FILMS— like *Salesman* (1969) about fast-talking Bible salesmen in the South, or Kenneth Anger's *Scorpio Rising*, about freewheeling motorcycle gangs—cinema verité films showing real people doing real things. Also, travelogues of exotic faraway lands, and wild life nature films such as Beaver Builds A Dam, etc.

EDUCATIONAL FILMS— specialized subject matter that can be used as teaching devices on particular themes, such as diet, anatomy, outer space, alcoholism, auto safety, venereal disease, the United Nations, etc.

NEWSREEL FILMS— direct eyewitness coverage of events in the real world, such as troops in combat, bathing beauty contests, public ceremonies, sports coverage, etc.

ANIMATION FILMS— cartoon characters such as Walt Disney's 1940 film of *Pinocchio*, based on Carlo Lorenzini's 1881 story, where Disney took 3 years and 80 musicians and 750 artists to create over one million drawings that went into a 450,000 frame, 88-minute film, etc.

SURREALIST FILMS— the dreamlike representation of unconscious imagery such as Jean Cocteau's *Blood of the Poet* (1932), which scrambles and intercuts reality sequences to show what is going on in the irrational psyche.

In addition to all of the above film types, there are also dozens of technical specialty types of film, such as computer graphics and holographic films that experiment in three dimensional and other visual and sound effects.

But no matter what type of film one is making—whether dramatic or lyric or epic feature film, or one of the more specialized types that are described above—there will always be two important principles which will differentiate film work from stage plays:

1. Film has more freedom of space and time than the stage. The stage is basically a fixed point of view, using units of time and space that are usually restricted to what is happening right here and now, whereas a camera will almost always use a moving point of view that keeps changing from place to place, and film will also use montage editing techniques to juxtapose time sequences and create flashbacks, time lapses and sudden leaps forward into the future.

2. Film tends towards extreme realism, whereas the stage tends towards more stylized representation. Another way of saying this is: the stage is about being big, whereas film is about being small. This is because the stage is dominated by the verbal word, whereas film is dominated by the visual image. As Otto Preminger puts it:

The camera demands reality and registers without mercy everything artificial. That's why a real room looks better on the screen than a set, even if it is an exact replica of that room. That's why the stage actor is at a disadvantage on the screen.[9]

Tennessee Williams says it another way: "We see representative props in a stage production, but in a film we have an image of the real thing itself." All you have to do is think of that tiny glass unicorn in *The Glass Menagerie* and you'll see what Williams is talking about—in the stage play it seems to be a poetic emblem for everything that is fragile and unearthly and ethereal, whereas in the film version it is simply an insignificant figurine which accidentally gets its horn broken off.

If film has more freedom of space and time than the stage, and if film also tends more towards extreme realism than the stage, then it follows that film acting will probably be noticeably different from stage acting.

And indeed it is. Acting in films is much closer to real behavior than it could ever be onstage. This explains the phenomenal success of a certain deadpan acting technique and classical understatement on the part of such excellent film actors as William S. Hart, Humphrey Bogart and Gary Cooper, who could achieve an extraordinary believability onscreen with their understatement but would never be able to get away with the same technique onstage. Henry Fonda is one of the few American actors whose underplaying was so skillful that he could command both the stage and the screen with his subdued but controlled performances.

This secret of film acting explains the preposterous claim made by John Ford, who called John Wayne "the best actor in Hollywood." Ford simply meant that John Wayne was always John Wayne, in everything he did, and therefore he was completely believable onscreen. John Wayne himself confirmed Ford's estimate when he made the modest, off-hand disclaimer: "How many times do I gotta tell ya? I don't *act* at all. I *re*-act." That is, John Wayne's acting was more like his own behavior in real life, than it was like anything you might find onstage.

Herbert Berghof, one of the great acting teachers of our time, is fond of saying that the best actor in films is Lassie, because she does everything instinctively so no one can ever catch her "acting" a part.

In *The Film Sense*, Eisenstein quotes George Arliss on the difference between stage and film acting:

> I had always believed that for the movies, acting must be exaggerated, but I saw in this one flash that *restraint* was the chief thing that the actor had to learn in transfering his art from the stage to the screen. The art of restraint and suggestion on the screen may any time be studied by watching the acting of the inimitable Charlie Chaplin.[10]

And Laurence Olivier in his autobiography describes the difference between stage acting and film acting, speaking of the period 1932–33:

> At that time, stage acting and film acting were thought of as two entirely different crafts, even professions. We know now that this is not by any means a true assessment: the truth is infinitely subtler. They call for the same ingredients but in different proportions. The precise difference may take some years of puzzling work to appreciate: in each case there are many subtle variations according to the character of the actor.[11]

Olivier is careful to leave the subtle variations up to the individual actor, but we could venture our own opinion as to the "different proportions" that are required in film acting.

Events that take place onstage will call for a greater projection than events that take place on film, because the stage has a fixed distance between actor and audience that has to be bridged by the actor's voice and his physical instrument. But the camera is more flexible and immediate, and does not require the actor to bridge anything except his own being.

And that explains an odd principle that every technical person is aware of on location—if an actor performs very movingly on the set, and if the technical crew is impressed by the scene and applauds the actor after a particular take, you can be pretty sure that that scene is not going to come off very well on film. Because we are not dealing here with a stage performance, but something infinitely more subtle—it may be more-important how this actor is moving his mouth, or the peculiar angle of his eyebrow, or the shadow on his left earlobe, than all the inner truth he may be projecting, no matter how well motivated. This sounds cuckoo, but that's simply the way it happens to be with cameras and film.

And this goes a long way towards explaining why film is more a director's medium than the stage is—it is not merely a matter of power or egoism or authority, it is more a technical consideration and concerns the very nature of film itself.

Onstage everything will depend on how the actor uses his total instrument—his voice, his body, his stage presence. Whereas onscreen everything depends on what a director chooses to show us—in a single take, the camera can focus on the actor's cheekbone or the back of his head or his profile, and that one positioning may be every bit as important as anything the actor may be saying or doing at the moment. It is the director's choice that will determine, finally, what appears up there on the movie screen.

Granted. But still, the screenwriter has his own control of the story line, which is a much deeper choice and power and authority, even, than the director's choice of camera positioning. Let's think again of the difference between film and stage plays. We said that film has more freedom of space and time than the stage has. In fact, film has more freedom of everything—freedom of image, detail, focus, distance, movement, action, theme, and choice of style and treatment.

Because the eye of the movie camera is free to range over each and every aspect of our physical universe, it can show how high white clouds accumulate across the sky, it can show the tiniest leaf tip and the loftiest mountain top, and it can show how deep sea creatures stumble along in their lumbersome slow motion going.

And within the range of human experience, the camera eye can record almost anything you can think of: a child off by himself pouting beside a chain wire fence in the corner of a grade school playground; two lovers taking their clothes off and standing face to face with each other for the first time; an old woman sitting alone by a window; a gang of leather jacketed teenagers mugging a middle-aged woman on a racing subway train; an airplane losing altitude suddenly and all the passengers in a cold panic; a man handing a note to a bank teller instructing her to pass over all the loose cash; a father and son arguing along the sea coast as the ocean beats furiously against the slippery glistening rocks; an actress waiting backstage for her entrance, thinking for an instant of her dead father who never saw her perform; a writer bending over his manuscript in the middle of the night, laboring patiently to get this one page exactly right; a terminal cancer patient lying in a hospital bed, waiting to see his wife for the last time; two farmboys having a fist fight behind the hay barn, black-eyed and bloody because they are both in love with the same girl.

Film offers us all these endless possibilities, and more, and these possibilities all belong to the screenwriter because he is the one who initiates the freedom of space and time and image and theme and action, in his original screenplay story line.

But this freedom comes with a price. The screenwriter cannot enjoy this enormous creative latitude of screenwriting, without realizing that every one of his screenplays must also engage the services of a whole host of other artists in the filmmaking process. So this entails a tremendous responsibility for the screenwriter.

He must realize that the business nature of the film

industry has reached such gargantuan proportions, that it is difficult to think of any other art form where the cost/profit factor will operate as relentlessly as it does in motion pictures. Orson Welles describes this inexorable condition of filmmaking:

> A typewriter needs only paper; a camera uses film, requires subsidiary equipment by the truckloads and several hundreds of technicians. That is always the central fact about the filmmaker as opposed to any other artist; he can never afford to own his own tools. The minimum kit is incredibly expensive; and one's opportunities to work with it are rather less numerous than might be supposed. In my case I've been given the use of my tools exactly eight times in twenty years.[12]

Certainly this is radically different from playwriting and stage work. Because even though Broadway productions have also become enormously expensive, that still doesn't prevent a playwright from writing his plays and then having them performed in some off-off-Broadway house in an Equity approved showcase. However, even a low-budget film will be far beyond the cost of an off-off-Broadway production, and as one leading screenplay agent comments:

> There are no non-profit films, as there are non-profit stage productions where actors are allowed to donate their services without fee on a showcase basis.[13]

So in exchange for the enormous freedom that a screen-writer is given to exercize in his medium, he must make himself aware of the commercial appeal of his work. That may sound crass and vulgar, but it happens to be a fact of the film industry. He is not merely creating art, he is also generating business. As Kenneth MacGowan once put it:

> When a fabled young woman like Audrey Hepburn expresses an interest in anything filmable . . . it has the

instant effect of lifting a work of literature to the status of a "property."[14]

One cannot underestimate the pressure of cost factor thinking in filmmaking. Stanley Kubrick describes how it affects his own work:

> You have a problem of allocating your resources of time and money in making a film, and you are constantly having to do a kind of artistic cost-effectiveness of all the scenes in the film against the budget and time remaining. This is not wholly unlike some of the thinking that goes into a chess game.[15]

Of course a screenwriter can become too obsessed with trying to calculate what will sell in the film industry. And the fact is, it's impossible to second-guess the market for films. William Goldman cautions the screenwriter against taking this too seriously:

> The greatest shibboleth that drives me crazy about the goddamned picture business is when somebody says, "Well I did that because I knew it was going to be commercial." No one has the least idea because you're guessing public taste three years down the line . . . I say this again and again and again . . . the basic truth of the movie business is nobody knows anything. Nobody knows anything. They say they know, but they don't know, they're guessing. It's all a guess. No one knows what will work, and that's why it's all a crap shoot.[16]

So the screenwriter should be concerned about the business nature of the film industry—but not overly concerned. It's a fine balance, and one that has to be learned by experience.

What else should the screenwriter know about the difference between writing filmscripts as opposed to writing stage plays? Only this: that the two art forms are in a very curious relation to one another.

Stage plays are often sold from Broadway to Hollywood, so there can be film versions made of what was originally intended for the stage. But we rarely hear of the opposite being the case—a Hollywood film being sold to Broadway, so there can be a stage version made of what was originally intended for the screen.

And the reasons for this are probably much deeper than the obvious economic ones, that there's more money to be made out of a successful film than can usually be made out of a successful stage play. Someone may say, it's also a chance to achieve a kind of artistic permanence by "fixing" the stage play in film form. And we can certainly be grateful that some great stage plays and stage performances have been preserved for us in film, the way Henry Fonda's masterful Broadway performance as *Mr. Roberts*, the navy lieutenant on a utility cargo ship who yearns for the reality of combat service, was "fixed" for all time in the excellent 1955 film version of the stage play.

But before we congratulate ourselves on the fact that film is always more permanent and more enduring than stage plays can ever be, we should remind ourselves that nothing is ever more enduring or more permanent than the text of a great stage play. *Oedipus Rex, Medea, Hamlet, Macbeth, King Lear*—these texts will survive all our feeble attempts to "fix" them in cinematic terms. And the reason for this is clear: the art of filmmaking is very young, a mere 90 years old —whereas stage plays have existed for over 2500 years, and they will always remain the noblest and most eloquent form of human expression.

When we think of the greatest stage plays, we invariably think of their authors: Aeschylus, Sophocles, Euripides; Shakespeare, Racine, Molière; Ibsen, Strindberg, Chekhov; O'Neill, Miller, Williams. These great stage playwrights all express their respective eras in a way that no film can—not yet, anyway.

However, that's not the case with certain other mixed

mediums that also derive from stage plays—like opera, where the author of the text is usually secondary. When we think of the operas of Mozart or Verdi or Puccini, we usually don't think about who wrote the book or the libretti for their operas—and chances are we would have no idea who wrote the texts for *The Magic Flute* or *Don Giovanni* or *Aida* or *Rigoletto* or *La Boheme* or *Tosca*. In fact, we'd probably be surprised to learn that Puccini's *Madame Butterfly* is based on a book by the famous New York impressario, David Belasco.

Film itself, like opera, is just such a mixed medium—it derives from stage plays, but it has its own independent and peculiar nature. On the one hand, the screenwriter of films is carrying on the heritage of the great stage playwrights; but on the other hand, the screenwriter will often seem to be as secondary and unsung as the librettist of a Verdi opera.

Nor is the screenwriter the only artist who may suffer some ambiguity in this mixed medium of film. Take the 1939 movie of *Gone with the Wind*, based on the novel by Margaret Mitchell. This epic story of the Civil War, Scarlett O'Hara and the burning of Atlanta, was produced by David O. Selznick, who was the chief moving force behind the film's execution and completion. During the shooting of the film, *Gone with the Wind* ran through three major directors—George Cukor, Victor Fleming, and Sam Wood. And it passed through the hands of a whole host of adapters and screenwriters —including F. Scott Fitzgerald and Ben Hecht. Yet the finished film emerges as an entirely new entity, not really the creation of any one of the directors or screenwriters. *Gone with the Wind* is uniquely itself, one of the most curiously successful collaborative efforts ever achieved in Hollywood.

So film does, indeed, have its roots in the great tradition of stage plays—but film is also such a hybrid mixed medium art form, that it will sometimes be difficult to recognize the work of the screenwriter in the way one can usually locate the work of the stage playwright.

To summarize: the screenwriter will have more freedom and place and time than the stage playwright has, and he can range over the whole universe for locations and images and actions that may suit his original screenplay story line. And the screenwriter will also be working in a medium that tends towards extreme realism, and so he will have to train himself to craft his screenplay accordingly. Film actors will usually be achieving their greatest effects by understating their actions, and the screenwriter must realize this as he is writing his screenplay. The actual process of filmmaking will usually be under the control and authority of one film director, much more than a stage play is—and the screenwriter had better be aware of this fact. Films will always be more closely bound to the economics and technical considerations of the industry, than a stage playwright will usually be bound to the commercial requirements of the theatre. And finally, the two art forms of stage plays and filmscripts are in a very curious relation to one another, having a great deal in common but also having radical differences.

The screenwriter must realize all these things, because they are all a part of the complex process of filmmaking.

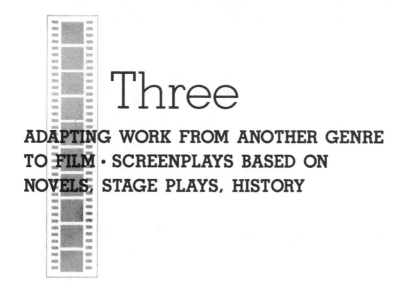

Three

ADAPTING WORK FROM ANOTHER GENRE TO FILM • SCREENPLAYS BASED ON NOVELS, STAGE PLAYS, HISTORY

Sometimes we feel a slight contempt for "adaptations," works which are derived from previously existing works. We feel somehow that they are not as valuable or meritorious or challenging as original works. And because of this, we tend to feel that anyone who works as an adapter is somehow a second-rate writer, not as authentic or talented or conscientious as someone who creates an entirely original work.

Yet if we knew more about the history of literature, we wouldn't feel so superior about adaptations. Most of the greatest work that has ever been done has been derived from previously existing materials.

All the greatest classical Greek plays—*Medea, Agamemnon, Oedipus Rex, Antigone, The Trojan Women, Prometheus Bound* —were all adaptations from much earlier myth stories of the Greek gods. And Aeschylus himself commented that all his own work was nothing but leftovers from the great banquet of Homer, the epic poet who composed the *Iliad* and the *Odyssey*.

And the same thing is true of almost all of Shakespeare's greatest plays—*Hamlet, Othello, King Lear, Macbeth, The Tempest, Romeo and Juliet, Henry V, Richard III*—the plots of all these great plays were either borrowed or adapted or plain stolen from previously existing works. In fact there is only one play by Shakespeare which is his own entirely original creation, with a plot and characters of his own devising, and that play is probably Shakespeare's least distinguished work —*The Merry Wives of Windsor*, which is the only play that is written entirely in prose.

So it's not surprising when we consider that most films are based on previously existing material. In fact it would be hard to think of a good film that is not based, in some way or other, on a preexisting novel or stage play or biography or history.

The problem of adaptation, then, is to develop an instinct for what will work in film terms and what will not.

There are a lot of great novels that simply would not translate well onto the screen. The novels of Franz Kafka are haunting in their remorseless sense of doom, and the novels of Marcel Proust are brilliant in their subtlety of perception, and the novels of James Joyce are overwhelming in their momentum of stream of consciousness. But the greatness of all these authors depends so much on their strong narrative genius for telling what they have to tell in a peculiar way, that it is not likely that any of these works could ever be successfully translated into screen terms without a profound loss.

And the problem becomes even more acute when we are dealing with first person novels. *Huckleberry Finn* is an outstanding example of a first person novel that depends on the colloquial dialect voice of Huck Finn as its first person narrator, and without that voice narrating the entire story line, *Huckleberry Finn* would seem like just another rustic slice of Americana without any special genius to raise it above any one of a hundred other stories. J. D. Salinger's *The Catcher in the Rye* is another example of a first person novel that would lose its poignancy if it were taken out of the first person voice of Holden Caulfield and made into a visual documentary of an adolescent's confusion over his sudden awareness of the ways of the adult world. And Kurt Vonnegut's *Slaughterhouse Five* has such a strong first person narrative in the novel, that it could never be adequately translated into film terms—even though the movie version of *Slaughterhouse Five* is an excellent film in its own right, it is simply not the same narrative voice as Kurt Vonnegut creates for us in the novel.

In addition, let's get one thing straight—it's not as simple as letting some actor read the narrative first person as a voice-over onto the sound track. In fact, that's usually the worst of all options. James Agee points out the inadequacy of this technique, in a 1945 review of *The Picture of Dorian Gray:*

> I wish somebody would take book lovers like Mr. W. Lewin aside and explain to them, once and for all, that to read from the text of a novel—not to mention interior monologues—when people are performing on the screen, while it may elevate the literary tone of the production, which I doubt, certainly and inescapably plays hell with it as a movie.[17]

The problem of translating narrative voice into cinematic terms is a complex difficulty, and not something to be solved by any easy solutions. In fact, it may raise some question as to whether the whole venture is at all worthwhile.

As great a screenwriter as Ingmar Bergman raises this question:

> There are many reasons why we ought to avoid trying to film all of existing literature—but the most important reason is that the irrational dimension, which is the heart of a literary work, is often untranslatable and that in its turn kills the special dimension of the film. If despite this we wish to translate something literary into filmic terms, we are obliged to make an infinite number

of complicated transformations which most often give limited or non-existent results in relation to the efforts expended.[18]

Even so, there have been adaptations of great novels that have managed to get around the problem of a strong narrative voice and still present a creditable film onscreen. The Hollywood version of *War and Peace* in 1956 was a three and a half hour adaptation of the epic novel of Napolean's invasion of Russia—Tolstoy's own extended narrative and occasional digressions on the philosophy of history were left out, and instead there was enormous spectacle and romance. It was a good enough job, even though it was certainly not the epic novel that Tolstoy wrote. Later in 1968, the Russians produced their own multi-million dollar version of *War and Peace*, under the direction of Sergei Bondarchuk, which ran for six and a half hours, and this version tried to present the entire novel, complete with Tolstoy's own narrative voice. It was a commendable effort, albeit rather exhausting to sit through.

More recently, certain adapters have managed to bring difficult novels to the screen with considerable success. One of our finest screen adapters, Horton Foote, did a number of the more complex Faulkner novels, as well as Harper Lee's *To Kill a Mockingbird* in 1962, and the more recent *Tender Mercies*.

The problem is by no means restricted to how novels can be made into film—there can be as many difficulties in trying to translate a great stage play into cinematic terms. George Bernard Shaw pinpoints this problem when he writes:

The film lends itself admirably to the succession of events proper to narrative and epic, but physically impracticable on the stage. *Paradise Lost* would make a far better film than Ibsen's *John Gabriel Borkman*, though Borkman is a dramatic masterpiece, and Milton could not write an effective play.[19]

The problem works in reverse, as well—as Erwin Panofsky comments, once one has written a decent screenplay, that is no reason to believe it will make for very interesting narrative reading:

> Good movie scripts are unlikely to make good reading and have seldom been published in book form: whereas, conversely, good stage plays have to be severely altered, cut, and, on the other hand, enriched by interpolations to make good movie scripts.[20]

Let's look very closely at what Panofsky is saying here: to make a good screenplay adaptation from another medium like a stage play, he says the screenwriter has to be prepared to *alter severely*, and also to *cut*, and also to *enrich by interpolations*. In other words, the screenwriter would be expected to rearrange certain sequences in the original, edit out certain other sections from the original, and also add some of his own materials to the original.

This seems to be a fair summary of what has come to be accepted as a license which any screenwriter has to have to adapt work from some other genre into good screenplay form: he must be allowed to rearrange, cut and add whatever he feels is necessary to make the material work in cinematic terms.

From one point of view, we can understand why the screenwriter must be given this liberty. Unless he is empowered to make whatever alterations and adjustments he feels are essential to render the material effective as a film, how else can he translate from one medium to another medium? Yet, while we can understand the need for this liberty, there is still something inside of us that cries out that all these changes are a sad betrayal of the original form of the work. In fact, this something inside of us sometimes even cries out that these changes are a profanation that should not be allowed to take place under any circumstances.

Good. That something that cries out inside of us has an excellent point, and we should always listen very carefully to it, and be exceedingly glad that it is there inside of us, because it's probably the closest we will ever come to having an artistic conscience in these matters.

41

In reality, though, that something that cries out inside of us strikes us as the voice of Innocence—which does not have much to say to the voice of responsible Experience. For example, let's assume that someone wants to make a film of *Moby Dick*—what would that voice of Innocence advise? That we shoot the whole novel, page by page, exactly the way Melville has written it? God forbid. All you have to do is pick up the novel and read through the first twenty or thirty pages and you'd realize the results of that approach. It would be disastrous, and any film that was ever made from any novel would be a catastrophe—and worse than that, it would also be a horrendous, crashing bore. There simply have to be some changes made if you want to translate *Moby Dick* into any kind of a decent, interesting film.

We can see the rightness of this approach if we look at the problem of translating something from one language to another. Here is the opening stanza of a short poem by Paul Verlaine, *Chanson D'Automne*—in the original French the lines are dreamlike, eerily nostalgic, and one of the most purely musical sounds imaginable:

> Les sanglots longues
> Des violons
>   De l'automne
> Blessent mon coeur
> D'une languer
>   Monotone.

Now—how would we go about translating this poem into English? Should we insist on a word-for-word literal translation from the French? That would give us something like the following:

> The sobbings long
> Of the violins
>   Of autumn
> Wound my heart
> With a languor
>   Monotonous.

That's fairly accurate on a literal level, but it reads like a pretty dumb poem. To say nothing of the fact that we've lost the three rhyme sequences of the original, and the strong metrical rhythm of iambic dimeter. And we've also botched the subtle nuance of feeling that derives from the diction of the original.

Does that mean that the poem itself can't be translated at all? Not necessarily, it just means that we're not going to get the job done to our satisfaction if we keep insisting on a literal word-for-word translation. However, if we allow ourselves a little license to rearrange and adjust some of the lines and phrases and words, perhaps we may be able to render the original French poem into an English equivalent that can save the rhyme scheme and the metric and also produce a poem that may be able to stand on its own in English.

Here's one possibility:

> The distant strings
> Of autumn brings
>   An old song
> Which hurts my heart
> With its dull art
>   Sad and long.

Notice we had to introduce the idea of "an old song" which is an interpolation on our part. And we rearranged the positioning of the word "autumn" from line three to line two. And we committed a deliberate grammatical error by treating "strings" as a collective singular, so it would go with the singular verb form "brings." Necessary adjustments, if we were going to work within such a tight rhyme scheme and still keep the meter and the meaning. But within the context of the poem, these adjustments and interpolations are hardly noticeable, and we've been reasonably successful in duplicating something of the simplicity and plaintiveness of the original French poem.

This is not to say that someone else might not come along and do it better, or at least, differently. All we are demonstrating here is that in order to do it at all, we have had to take a few liberties of rearrangement and adjustment with the original. Our artistic conscience has not been very seriously violated—at least we can live with ourselves, although we're under no illusion that what we were able to achieve comes close to the genius of the original poem by Verlaine. But at least our version is a few cuts above the literal word-for-word translation we began with.

Perhaps now we can see why film producers defend their practice of altering a work that exists in another genre, before it is even put in screenplay form. There are always going to be changes that will have to be made to adjust any work from its original medium to the very special technical requirements of film.

Otto Preminger talks of this, with reference to his film *Exodus* which was based on the novel by Leon Uris, which Dalton Trumbull adapted as a screenplay:

> People often come to me and ask if the film is going to be faithful to the book. "Faithful to the book." Once an author sells (and "sells" is a very hard word) the film rights, he gives up any claim to have somebody do it "faithfully".[21]

Of course, Preminger argues, he will have to bring as much integrity as he can to the adaptation—but conscience aside, the original material will still have to go through a process of translation before it can be turned into worthwhile film material:

> When I prepare a story for filming it is being filtered through my brain, my emotions, my talent such as I have. Some characters don't interest me so I drop them, others who are minor in the book appeal strongly to me and I develop them to become more attractive. I may create new characters altogether. I have no obligation, nor do I try, to be "faithful" to the book.[22]

Of course, whenever any liberty or license is given to anyone, there will always be the possibility of making some pretty dreadful mistakes. The reader can probably think of any number of excellent novels that were made into atrocious films, due to inept or incompetent adaptations. Tennessee Williams is on record as saying that the film version of *The Glass Menagerie* was a preposterous misreading of his intentions in the original stage play:

> The most awful travesty of the play I've ever seen . . .
> horribly mangled by the people who did the film-
> script . . .[23]

Williams felt the most grievous error in the film adaptation was to give the story a "happy ending," and he also felt that the characterizations were grotesquely distorted. And he felt a great actress like Gertrude Lawrence deserved a much better screenplay than the one she was given for the role of Amanda Wingfield.

Still, there are screenplay adaptations that are done with conscience, intelligence, and sensitivity. Such an adaptation took place in the 1940 film version of *The Grapes of Wrath*, by John Steinbeck. Nunnally Johnson wrote the film version, and he was told that he was free to do anything he wanted with the original Steinbeck novel:

> He said, in effect, "Look. If it doesn't violate the book,
> do whatever you want. I'll promise you that John won't
> object, because he knows enough to know that this is
> another medium." I didn't hesitate, after that, to switch
> things around, or switch speeches around.[24]

Granted, then, that the screenwriter has license to make alterations and changes and interpolations in an original work—what are the general guiding principles for making screenplay adaptations from another genre?

The best answer to that question can be given by several outstanding screenwriters who have made successful adaptations from other mediums. We'll look at statements by Nunnally Johnson, who adapted *The Grapes of Wrath* by John Steinbeck; Ray Bradbury, who adapted *Moby Dick* by Herman Melville; and William Goldman, who adapted *All the President's Men* from a factual book by Carl Bernstein and Bob Woodward.

Nunnally Johnson reports how he went about making the adaptation of *The Grapes of Wrath*:

> I have learned to look for the backbone, the skeleton of a novel, what this fellow was setting out to tell, so that actually he could have told it in a nightletter. Almost. John Steinbeck wanted to tell, in *The Grapes of Wrath*, what an act of nature did to a great segment of helpless people and how they reacted. Not only that, because that would just be a tract, but he created human beings—Ma and Pa and Grampa and Preacher and Rosasharn. That's a tremendously impressive thing to think of, (and) I had to read the book two or three times before it all became clear to me, like an X-ray photograph. You know, the bones became visible.[25]

Ray Bradbury reports on his approach to *Moby Dick* by Herman Melville:

> When you adapt another person's book, it's got to get into your bloodstream so completely that it can come out on an emotional level and be recreated. It has to be recreated through your emotions and not rethought. Your emotions will do the rethinking for you . . .[26]

And William Goldman reports on his approach to adapting *All the President's Men* by Woodward and Bernstein:

> What one tries to do in an adaptation is, two things: First of all, ad nauseum you try to find what is the spine

of the piece. Plus, you have to think what was it that thrilled you? What was the pleasure that the book gave you, or the play gave you, or the story or the article? What moved you? What moved you? Now, you have to combine those two things somehow. You have to keep those elements that were moving . . . either to laughter or to tears. Plus keeping the story straight.[27]

All of these statements by these outstanding screenwriters can be summarized as follows:

1. Try to make the original work a part of your own nervous system, your own emotional life, so you will become the author of the new work that will be born out of the adaptation.

2. Look for the spine, the skeleton, the backbone, the summary statement of the novel or history or biography or prose piece you are trying to adapt.

Of course this takes a tremendous amount of homework and conscientious concentration—reading and rereading of the original material, and then allowing it to settle into one's own unconscious, to see what one's deepest response to it will be—and then trying to locate the essential structure of the work so one can say it to oneself in the simplest possible terms. It sounds easy, but of course it will call forth all one's powers of creativity and reflection.

We can put all of this to a test, by trying to make a short screenplay adaptation of a very brief scene from a stage play. We'll choose one of the shortest scenes in all dramatic literature—the opening scene of *Macbeth* by William Shakespeare.

Here is the original brief scene, as it appears in Act One, scene one, of *Macbeth:*

SCENE ONE - a desert Heath.

Thunder and lightning. Enter three Witches.

> FIRST WITCH: When shall we three meet again
> In thunder, lightning, or in rain?

> SECOND WITCH: When the hurly burly's done,
> When the battle's lost and won.

> THIRD WITCH: That will be ere the set of sun.

> FIRST WITCH: Where the place?

> SECOND WITCH: Upon the heath.

> THIRD WITCH: There to meet with Macbeth.

> FIRST WITCH: I come, Graymalkin!

> SECOND WITCH: Paddock calls.

> THIRD WITCH: Anon.

> ALL: Fair is foul and foul is fair:
> Hover through the fog and filthy air.

EXEUNT

Only thirteen short lines to create the major action and theme and atmosphere of the entire play! The witches are on and off in a wild flurry of evil excitement, startling the audience into an awareness that foul things are afoot and fair things may turn foul at a moment's notice.

So. The first thing that we have to do with this brief scene, is read it over and over and over. We may think we see what is going on, but on each rereading we will discover more things that are happening. So we challenge the reader to go back right now and reread the brief scene, over and over, before proceeding any further with our discussion about how to make an adequate screenplay adaptation of it. Go on, go back and reread the scene, right now.

A thorough rereading of the scene should reveal that the first witch doesn't really know what is going on, she's the one that has to ask twice for information about their next meeting. And the second and third witches are the ones who know what is really going on—not only with their next meeting, but also with the day's events—they seem to have foreknowledge of how the battle will go, and when it will be decided. And a really careful rereading of the scene would reveal that it is the second witch who knows more than any of the others, as she is the one who is the most specific and detailed in her answers.

A thorough rereading of the scene would also reveal that the three witches probably enter from separate directions, and they will probably also exit in different directions, where they will each "hover" over separate areas of the battlefield until they come together again, on the heath, to meet with Macbeth.

Another curious fact—these witches do not seem to be able to move around independently—they are drawn to each other for quick violent meetings, and then they are just as quickly called away again by invisible offstage spirits which are calling to them.

Several readings and rereadings of the scene will reveal these details, and a host of other things that are happening. And the screenwriter's job is simply to find out what is there, right there in front of him, in the scene, before he begins making any adaptation of it.

Our challenge now is to try to translate this brief scene into a filmscript adaptation. We may not be able to please everyone with the choices that we will make, but at least we will be true to the facts of the scene as we have uncovered them by several close rereadings. And we will be able to demonstrate the appropriate screenplay format that our adaptation ought to have.

Since this is such a brief scene, thank heaven we won't have to cut or edit or rearrange any of the spoken lines, and that's always a relief when we're dealing with a text that we respect. However, if this scene were any longer than it is, we wouldn't hesitate to trim it down, and edit out a few lines here and there, in order to stay as close as possible to the spine of the central action.

All we have to do with this scene, then, is try to open it up

49

in cinematic terms. This means we will have to provide a running narrative with stage directions that will give just enough suggestive detail description so we can stimulate the imagination of a producer and a director, to render the scene in specific visual terms. And we will also have to hint at how the dialogue should be spoken, since that is not provided in the original text. And finally, we will have to indicate the correct sequencing of camera shots that will have to be made.

Here is our screenplay adaptation of the scene:

FADE IN ON:

EXTERIOR

A desert heath. Dark gray cloud shapes overhead —rumbling thunder, brilliant flashes of bright lightning. Below, the aftermath of a late morning battle—broken swords, armor pieces strewn across the ground, and lifeless bodies lying motionless. Here and there a body occasionally lifts an arm in the air, then collapses backwards to the earth.

CUT TO:

Bare space before an enormous grotesque oak tree. FIRST WITCH suddenly appears from nowhere, looks around frantically, as if searching for something, someone. Just as suddenly, SECOND and THIRD WITCHES appear from nowhere—warty, scabrous, dyspeptic, they look like bad scabs of a sad past, a trio of raggedy bag ladies who are out to gather spoils from the day's battle.

> FIRST WITCH (*cries out*): When shall we three meet again—
> In thunder, lightning, or in rain?

> SECOND WITCH (*quickly*): When the hurly burly's done,
> When the battle's lost and won.

> THIRD WITCH (*knowing*): That will be ere the set of sun.

> FIRST WITCH (*still frantic*): Where the place?

> SECOND WITCH: Upon the heath.

> THIRD WITCH: There to meet with Macbeth.

Pause. ALL THREE WITCHES freeze in place, as if something had suddenly happened.

FIRST WITCH (*answering a call from offscreen*): I come, Gray-malkin!

SECOND WITCH (*also answering call from offscreen*): Paddock calls.

THIRD WITCH (*signalling to other two*): Anon.

PULL BACK TO REVEAL:

Entire heath with witches now reduced in size to twig figures as they join arms and do quick jerky dance as they chant:

ALL Fair is foul and foul is fair:
Hover through the fog and filthy air.

Suddenly FIRST WITCH disappears into nowhere, and just as suddenly the SECOND and THIRD WITCH also disappear, as

SLOW

DISSOLVE

As we said, the reader may agree or disagree with certain choices we have made, it doesn't much matter. The important thing is that we tried to render an adaptation that was faithful to the facts of the scene as we perceived them, and we provided enough technical information to allow a producer and a director to get some sense of what the film version would look like.

Now the reader can notice two very important things about our screenplay adaptation:

1. Because of its special layout format, our screenplay adaptation is almost three times as long as the original stage play scene. Actually there's no telling how the film

51

time would compare with the stage time of the two versions, because a lot would depend on the directors and how they chose to control the pace of the scene. But it's probably fair to say that the film version would run longer than the stage version, if only because of the camera's ability to show us so much more of the background—all that overhead sky with its dark gray cloud shapes, and then there would be pan shots of the battlefield—things one would see onstage at a glance, but on film would have to take a sequencing of different film images.

2. Just as Shakespeare always uses a minimum of stage directions, so we've tried to use a minimum of explicit camera indications, as that would intrude on the work of the director. Even so, we did imply a good deal of mobility on the part of the camera, and we also implied considerable intercutting that could be done from shot to shot. However, the specific choices of how to make each camera shot, and how to cut from one shot to another, is always a matter for the director and the cameraman and the film editor to determine. All the screenwriter needs to do is lay down the broad canvas of the scene as well as he can, and leave it at that.

As we said, this matter of making a screenplay adaptation from another genre looks easy enough, but once one faces into the responsibility of trying to translate something into film terms, it becomes as creative and all-absorbing as if one were trying to write one's own original screenplay.

Now as a final challenge, the reader can try making his own screenplay adaptation from some material taken from another genre.

Here is the simplest of nursery rhymes:

> Mary had a little lamb,
> Its fleece was white as snow;
> And everywhere that Mary went,
> The lamb was sure to go.

The reader is challenged to write a brief screenplay adaptation of this simple four line rhyme. This will mean, first, that he will have to go back and read and reread the piece, over and over again, until he has discovered as many facts that can be established as possible. Then he must try to create his own screenplay adaptation, staying as close as possible to the facts and the spirit of the original. He should also bear in mind the following important points of view:

1. the film director
2. the producer who is concerned with the budget
3. the actress playing the part of Mary
4. the lamb
5. the cameraman
6. the lighting man
7. the film editor
8. the music director
9. the art director

This may sound flippant, but it's not—we're deadly serious. If one can't make a decent screenplay adaptation out of something as basic as "Mary had a little lamb," there's no point in talking about trying to make a worthwhile screenplay adaptation of Homer's *Odyssey*.

Four

WRITING ORIGINAL SCREENPLAYS · STORY LINES · ACTIONS · VISUALS · TITLES

Now we come to how the screenwriter should go about trying to write his own original screenplay, and how he should develop his feelings and thoughts through the earliest stages of shaping his own cinematic story line.

First the screenwriter should have his own original idea for a screenplay, something he knows will make for a strong and interesting film. And he may get this original idea from anywhere—from his reading, or from seeing other films, or from some life experience he has had, or from a story that someone once told him, or from something he has come on in his own imaginings.

This idea may come to him anywhere at all, and at any time, and in any way at all—haphazardly, as he is walking down a city street, or as he is lying in bed just before falling asleep, or as he is listening to someone talking about something that may be completely unrelated to anything, or while he is working on some other project. There are no rules for creative inspiration—it has to happen when and where it happens, and all that's really needed is for someone to train himself to pay attention to what is going on inside his own head, so he will be ready to receive the right idea at the right time, instead of overlooking it or casting it aside as not worth any further thought. Sometimes our best ideas may come as trivial flashes that any ordinary person would pass over as inconsequential. A leaf falls from a tree, a dog barks at a car, a bird flies over an old dirt road—all of these things might trigger an idea in the mind of the screenwriter that could have monumental significance, if he is only attentive enough to seize on it and see where it wants to go.

To be open for that first hint, that first glimpse of an idea that might get one into a strong story line—that's what's needed for the screenwriter to get started on his own original screenplay.

Neil Simon describes this experience of openness:

A fleeting moment goes by and I say, hey, that would make an idea for a play. That would make an idea for a movie. Sometimes it's as simple as just sitting down and thinking, without the slightest idea of what it is that I'm gonna write about, and I could just sit in this chair for hours with a pad and a pencil and say, What is it you want to write about?[28]

About the only thing a screenwriter should stay away from in these cases is something that he doesn't really know anything about. We don't mean just surface details—one can always read up on horses, or race cars, or airplanes, or whatever else a story line may be about. We mean in a deeper sense—there may be some subjects the screenwriter has no business trying to write about, because he has no background or inclination for it. For example, if someone has spent an entire lifetime trying to avoid anything that has to do with boxing because one has a strong distaste for it, then it would probably be foolish for this person to set out to write a screenplay about the life of Joe Louis, because he'd have to end up bluffing his way through every page of the screenplay. But then again, one never knows—the person's strong distaste for boxing may have been masking over a deep affinity for it which he had been repressing all his life. In this case it simply means that he has to get to know himself a lot better before he can judge which subject actions he ought to stay away from.

As we said, there are no rules for creative inspiration.

But let's assume that the screenwriter does manage to get hold of an idea that he thinks will make for a strong original story line. And let's say he feels pretty sure that he can follow through on whatever research he may have to do in order to get to know the subject area as well as he ought to know it. The next step, then, will be to develop the life of the characters who will be a part of the story line.

Getting to know one's characters may involve a good deal of time. Sometimes the screenwriter will have to put himself inside each character so he can experience the story line from the character's point of view—otherwise the characters will remain a lot of deadwood stick figures which the screenwriter will be pushing around to fit into some preconceived plot, and that will always end up as nothing but lifeless dry writing.

There are several different techniques for getting to know one's characters. Alvin Sargent, the screenwriter of *Paper Moon*, describes one approach:

I like to take each character and deal with him alone. Not for the script necessarily, but just as an exercise. I put them in a restaurant, a restroom, at home, in bed at night, lost in Alaska.[29]

This sounds like the improvisational work that an actor might do to try to get inside a character—imagining a lot of different circumstances that a character might be faced with, to see how the character would handle it. It's a playful and imaginative approach, and it doesn't always have to relate strictly to the story line—one is simply exercising, improvising, letting oneself play with the character in order to get to know him as well as one can.

One can use this same approach, but do it more strictly and more scrupulously, by writing it all down in a notebook.

Merian Cooper, the producer for John Ford on many films, describes using this technique during the filming of *Fort Apache:*

> On all my pictures I always write the history of each character from birth to death. If you do this, when you get someone playing the characters you know all about them: What country they came from, what their lives had been, what they ate, how they slept, whom they loved, whom they hated, how they died. There were eighteen characters, I think, in *Fort Apache*, that Jack and I did that way. Ford did more than me, I guess.[30]

It's very sobering to realize that the production people of a film—the producer and the director—will go to such extraordinary lengths to create the minute intimate details about the background of each character. Knowing that, the screenwriter shouldn't feel that it's asking too much of him to make a similar effort to get to know all of his characters as well as he possibly can.

In his *Memoirs*, Tennessee Williams describes another approach for getting to know his characters. Williams describes how, in the act of writing, he would get up and begin walking around a room, speaking out loud in the voice of each character, trying to find the precise intonation and diction and word choice that each character would hit on to say a particular thing. That is to say, Williams not only imagined the life of each character—he actually *became* the life of each character. That way, he would get so deeply inside each character that he would know exactly what the character would think and feel about something. Williams claims that was how he wrote Blanche Du Bois' famous line at the end of *A Streetcar Named Desire*, where she says as she is being led offstage by the doctor:

> Whoever you are—I have always depended on the kindness of strangers.

Williams actually found himself saying the line to himself, as if he were Blanche Du Bois being taken away by the doctor. Of course this approach means that in order to act out the various characters one is trying to write about, one has to strip away all vestiges of inhibition and self-consciousness. If the screenwriter isn't able to enter into the reality of his own characters, it's not likely that an audience will be able to.

Once a screenwriter has an idea of a strong original story line, and after he has taken the time to get inside the life of all of the characters, the next step will be to develop the actions of his story line.

Actions—what are they, exactly? Actions aren't the same thing as "business" or things that one does with one's hands or one's body—those are just external things that don't have anything to do with real character actions. Actions happen inside, they are what takes place when a character wants something, actions are what the characters have to have. Every character always has to have a strong action—that is, he has to want something. And whatever it is that the character wants, that will be his action, his objective, the one thing that he has to have.

There can be many different kinds of actions—there can be a discovery action, where someone wants to find out the truth about something or someone; there can be a seduction action, where someone wants to persuade someone else to do something; there can be a revenge action, where someone wants to get even with someone about something; there can be an escape action, where someone wants to get the hell away from someone or some place. These are the most frequent actions that occur in most drama, and there can be many other kinds of action—but any one of these actions will be enough to motivate a single character throughout the course of an entire screenplay.

But obviously, if one has several different characters all interacting in a screenplay, each one of the characters will have to have his own strong separate action. That means the characters will inevitably come into conflict with each other as they pursue the various things that they want. And it is

59

this conflict, this inevitable struggle that will exist among the different characters as they try to achieve their separate objectives, which creates the plot and tension of the story line.

Tension—that's always the result of how much is at stake for each of the characters. The more each character cares about his or her action, the more that is riding on a character's achieving his or her objective, the more an audience will care about the character. But if a character doesn't care very much about his action, if he is indifferent or undecided about his objective, then no audience will ever take him very seriously or be very concerned about him. Think about it—even the most comic characters, such as the sad tramp that Chaplin created, these characters are at their funniest when they seem to care the most about what their actions are. Charlie Chaplin getting ready to eat his own shoe in *The Gold Rush* is hilariously funny because he seems to be taking his action so seriously. And obviously, because the stakes are so high, there is a lot of comic tension in the scene—it is life or death for that poor bedraggled lost soul who has been reduced by circumstances to eating his own shoe.

We can lay it down as a general rule, then, that all characters have to have strong actions that they care about. Even psychotics and sleepwalkers have to have actions that they themselves believe are important, even though these actions may seem lunatic to an outside observer. The only thing that is not allowed in any film or stage play, is for a character to be boring—which is the same as saying, a character who does not much care about his or her action. Anything else goes, and of course the ideal is where all of the characters are giving and receiving actions from each other, and where there is a great deal at stake for all of the actions.

Let's take an example—suppose John wants to marry Mary. If John doesn't much care whether he does or doesn't succeed in his objective of marrying Mary, then we in the audience won't much care about what happens. But if John believes that his very life depends on his marrying Mary, then that action becomes the most important thing in the world for him, and we in the audience will also become very interested in finding out what happens to John's action, whether or not he gets to marry Mary.

Now suppose Mary doesn't particularly want to marry John, suppose she'd rather marry Harry—that creates an obstacle to John's getting what he wants. So then John's action has to be strong enough to overcome the obstacle of Harry, or else there will be no marriage, therefore no strong story line.

Now—how would we express all this visually, in film terms? Perhaps John has gone out and bought an expensive engagement ring which he wants to give to Mary—that ring will become the visual embodiment of John's action, and when we see how the engagement ring is treated in the course of the story line, then we'll know whether John's action is advancing towards its objective.

Of course, if we were telling this story for the stage, we'd probably have to confine the plot to one or two fixed places, over one or two specific periods of time. John might love Mary in Philadelphia during the summer of 1980, and we'd have to show this in two or three basic sets.

But onscreen we don't have such fixed limitations in our use of time and place, so we could tell the story using any number of locations and time sequences. The story might still take place in Philadelphia, but we could also intercut from other locations to show something about John's past life in Albany, and that might help to explain why he wants to marry Mary so much. And we wouldn't be restricted to staying in any one specific time period either, so we could introduce flashbacks from John's childhood that might be helpful in showing why he wants to marry Mary so much. We might even want to introduce a series of events that were taking place at the same time—we could show more of Mary's relationship with Harry, and a few other things that Mary was up to, which might help to explain why she isn't all that interested in marrying John.

This greater freedom of time and place is what film is all

about, and a large part of the skill of screenwriting is learning how to use this freedom to the best possible advantage.

And because film is primarily a visual medium, the important thing is to keep translating the actions of the various characters into visual terms—as we did with John's buying the expensive engagement ring. In fact, we could challenge ourselves to come up with sharp clear visuals that would embody the major actions of all of the characters —Mary and Harry and whoever else might figure in the story line. Visuals are extraordinarily important for the screenwriter to put right into the text of his screenplay, because all the brilliant dialogue and plotting and characterization in the world will not take the place of one strong visual which embodies the major action of a character.

Here are a few examples of outstanding visuals which embody the major action of a particular character:

1. In *The Caine Mutiny* (1954), based on Herman Wouk's novel, Captain Queeg carries a pair of steel balls in his coat pocket which he always pulls out and manipulates obsessively whenever he becomes distraught. These steel balls are visuals which embody the strong psychological action of Queeg's wanting people to know that he is the victim of an imaginary conspiracy.

2. In *Cat on a Hot Tin Roof* (1958), based on Tennessee Williams' stage play, Brick hobbles around on a crutch and keeps drinking himself into a blind stupor. The crutch and the alcohol are both visual embodiments of Brick's action, which is to avoid facing the truth about himself.

3. In *Psycho* (1960), at the end of the film we see the young man, Norman, sitting alone in a psychiatric ward, and as the camera zooms in for a close-up of his face, for one hideous split instant—about one or two frames of film —there is the superimposed image of the mother's skull face on the young man's face. This visual brilliantly

reveals the young man's action, which is the same as his mother's action—to become one with the other.

All of these visuals say more—and say it more eloquently —than any number of pages of well-written dialogue could possibly say about the actions of the characters in these films.

Once the screenwriter has come this far—once he has his idea, and his characters, and their actions, and their visuals all clearly in mind—the next step is to decide on the exact story line.

We'd better be very sure we know what we mean by that word "story." A story is not a lot of loosely thrown together episodes that don't add up to a cohesive whole—that's more in the order of an "episodic" plot that keeps dragging itself out endlessly and goes nowhere.

E. M. Forster gave a good working definition of "story" when he said it was a narrative of events arranged in their time sequence. Narrative—the telling of what things took place, put together in their correct chronological order, with a beginning and a middle and an end.

That sounds simple enough—just tell a story, as well as you can, about something that happened, and be sure that you get it in its proper time sequence. And it is simple, if it's done the way it ought to be done. But watch out for all the traps one can fall into.

One trap the screenwriter can fall into is thinking that a good story is made up of a lot of terrific dialogue. Not that good dialogue isn't excellent and necessary, because it is. The best kind of dialogue will be the verbal equivalent of the spine of the story line. But the worst thing one can do in writing a screenplay is to worry about whether one is going to be writing good dialogue. That's putting the cart before the horse, and it can make for ruinous screenwriting. William Goldman comments:

The important thing about a screenplay. Screenplays are not dialogue. Screenplays are structure. Screenplays are structure, that's all they are. They are structure. They are basic . . . certainly dialogue is helpful, certainly literate dialogue is pleasant, certainly funny dialogue is fun . . . but the reality is, the reason we can't quote many lines of dialogue besides "Frankly my dear, I don't give a damn," is because the dialogue doesn't matter that much. Obviously good dialogue is better than inept dialogue at any time, but for the most part, you have to have the scene that is in its proper place in the structure of the piece.[31]

Imagine that—here is the screenwriter who wrote *Butch Cassidy and the Sundance Kid* which had all that stunning dialogue, and he is telling us that dialogue doesn't matter all that much! But we'd better pay attention to him, because he happens to be right. The structure or the spine of the story line is what the screenwriter has to stay close to at all times—that is what screenwriting is all about. Dialogue comes afterwards, it comes as a consequence of staying close to the spine of the story line. And if it doesn't happen that way then the dialogue is just a lot of clever writing but it doesn't have much to do with what's really going on in the screenplay.

Another trap that the screenwriter can fall into in telling his story, is to overload his screenplay with a lot of exposition. Exposition, facts, background information on what the heroine had for breakfast or what the hero is carrying in his left hip pocket or what happened a week ago last Tuesday —that's all irrelevant to getting down to the real business of the story line. Exposition is boring and meaningless when it's only a preamble to telling the story that has to be told. The best way to handle exposition is to look at the work of our greatest playwrights and screenwriters—people like Shakespeare, Ibsen, Chekhov, Tennessee Williams, Arthur Miller and Edward Albee—and see how skillfully they handle this delicate matter of exposition. Almost always, these writers will plunge you right into the middle of a situation, and then subtly provide whatever background facts are really needed to explain what's going on. Think of that opening scene of *Macbeth*—before you get a chance to figure out what's going on, there are three witches onstage in the middle of a battlefield and they're making a date to meet with someone named Macbeth. We're thrown into the story line before we have a chance to find out what it's all about. And that's all right, because a few scenes later there will be all the necessary background information that we need to bring us up to date on what's going on.

Once one is telling the story, writing the screenplay, trying to keep the ongoing momentum of the actions of all the various characters, a screenwriter may occasionally run into stone walls and blind spots, and when that happens he can always rely on a few simple techniques. One useful exercise is to sit down and try paraphrasing the entire story line in a single paragraph. Once one can boil it all down to its simplest terms, put it in "Once upon a time" form so one can say it to someone else, one will be well on his way towards overcoming any snag or difficulty in getting back into the writing process. Carl Foreman, the screenwriter of *High Noon* and *Young Man with a Horn*, advocates this approach:

If you can't tell the story to yourself in a paragraph, then you're in terrible trouble. And if you can't tell it to someone else in a paragraph, you're in trouble. At least one should be able to get it down to its bare bones, and be able to say what it is, who it's about, what it's for, what it's meant to do, in one paragraph, to anyone.[32]

One final consideration about a screenwriter scripting his own original screenplay—he should always try to be aware of the budget that will be required for the shooting of his filmscript. There will be an enormous difference if he is scripting something along the scale of Star Wars, complete with missile silos and interplanetary systems and space age technology, or if he is simply scripting a powerful domestic saga that could be filmed very easily on Bleecker Street. Not that the screenwriter should become overly obsessive or fixated on the cost factor, but he should simply be aware that there may be a lot more difficulties in selling a screenplay that calls for a cast of 30,000 and the planet Neptune, than there will be with a screenplay with a small cast and reasonably modest production values.

What else?—well, one always has to think of an appropriate title for one's screenplay. The best titles are not simply tacked on or used as handles to carry a screenplay around with, nor do good titles have to be anything extraordinarily clever or catchy. Sometimes it's best to simply use the name of the major character if that character happens to embody the most important action of the story line, as it does in these films:

> *Mildred Pierce* (1945)
> *Saint Joan* (1957)
> *Elmer Gantry* (1960)
> *Hud* (1963)
> *Elvira Madigan* (1967)

On the other hand, if the most important action of the story line is not embodied in any of the major characters, but rather in some underlying motif or theme of the film, then the title should try to hint or indicate what this underlying theme is—as the following film titles do:

> *A Place in the Sun* (1951)
> *Summer and Smoke* (1961)
> *The Miracle Worker* (1962)
> *Long Day's Journey into Night* (1963)
> *Who's Afraid of Virginia Woolf?* (1966)

Neil Simon reports that the choice of the right title is an important part of his total experience of writing:

I spend a lot of time on the titles . . . Hopefully they come as soon as I think of the play, because it means I have a very clear understanding of what the play is about . . . *The Odd Couple* was one that came to me right away. *Prisoner of Second Avenue* . . . when you say *Prisoner of Second Avenue* you get an image, that's what I look for. When they don't come right away, I spend a great deal of time on them. Sometimes I like to look for titles that are already part of the language, because then when they are spoken everyone thinks they're talking about the play.[33]

To summarize—the screenwriter who wants to write his own original screenplay will need to begin with a powerful idea for a strong cinematic story line; then he will have to get to know the characters in this story; then he will want to develop the actions of these characters, and he will try to translate all these actions into sharp clear visuals that can be shown onscreen; then he will have to decide on his exact story line, avoiding the traps of too much dialogue or exposition; and then, he will try to gauge the budget requirements of his screenplay so he can keep it within reasonable limits. Finally, he will search for precisely the right title that will express what the original screenplay is all about.

Five

DEVELOPING A FILM HEAD ·
LEARNING TO USE A CAMERA ·
MONTAGE AND FILM EDITING

The most important thing for a screenwriter is to develop a film head—to begin to see and feel and experience reality in film terms.

Someone with a film head will always be making imaginary movies, wherever he is—on a crowded crosstown city street, looking down out of an airplane window, or sitting in a crowded room with different clusters of people all talking to each other. During each of these scenes, the person with a film head will be unconsciously setting up various camera angles, trying to decide which point of view will be the most effective to take in the whole scene, perhaps even doing a little imaginary intercutting from one sequence to another, to make the best film record of whatever it is he is experiencing at the moment.

This may sound a little cuckoo, but a screenwriter has to have this kind of a film head if he wants to learn how to work seriously in cinematic terms.

There are lots of ways to cultivate a film head. Some

people can acquire a strong filmic sense by going to museums and studying the great portraiture and landscape painters—the work of such masters as Raphael, Rembrandt, Durer, Dore, Daumier, Goya, Van Gogh, Gauguin, Cezanne, and Degas. There is no telling what a close consideration of the use of line, contrast, and composition may do for the imagination of a budding filmmaker. The great Russian pioneer Sergei Eisenstein derived the inspiration for many of his classic films by studying images on ancient Japanese scrolls.

Other people develop a strong filmic sense by studying the work of the great still photographers—their use of camera angles, stark lighting effects and bold approach to subject matter. Beginning with those haunting Civil War photographs of Matthew Brady, one can move through the twentieth century master photographers such as Steichen, Cartier-Bresson, Diane Arbus, and Walker Evans.

Other people can cultivate a film head by simply going out and seeing as many films as possible—not only recent releases, but also the great classic motion pictures such as *All Quiet on the Western Front, Citizen Kane, High Noon, On the Waterfront, Psycho,* and *The Godfather.* Most major cities have film theatres that specialize in showing revivals of old films, and some film schools and libraries arrange regular screenings from their archives. And once one has found a particular great film that one admires intensely, one can always go back and see the same film over and over again, until one has figured out everything there is to figure out about how the whole thing has been put together.

Neil Simon recalls his earliest experience of seeing films:

I remember as a child going to see Chaplin films, laughing so hard that I hurt—really, really hurt—and afraid to look up at the screen because that man was still doing that same thing that was hurting me so much and I wanted him to stop it, and yet I didn't want him to stop it.[34]

This statement beautifully expresses someone's profound early love for the experience of seeing movies, and we can feel how it must have an ongoing effect on the screenwriter's attitude towards film and filmmaking up to the present time.

There are other ways for the screenwriter to keep seeing as many films as possible. The chief value of a television set for a screenwriter is the opportunity to watch late night films from the 1940s and the 1950s and the 1960s. If one can adjust to the reduced field of vision on the ordinary TV tube, and if one can put up with all the asinine commercial interruptions, one can learn a good deal about how feature films were put together during the major studio era of filmmaking. And with the advent of home videocassette machines which can be plugged into one's own television set, a whole new opportunity opens up for a screenwriter to view his favorite films in the privacy of his own home. Plus, home videocassettes of feature films have the added advantage of allowing the viewer to stop and start them at any given point—you can go back and rerun certain scenes over and over again, until you have figured out all the techniques that went into making them particularly good or bad scenes.

There is another way for the screenwriter to cultivate a film head, and that is for him to go out and buy a camera and begin taking pictures for himself.

There are some 80 million camera owners in the world today, and most of them are deeply committed to the craft of photography, with all its obsessive shop talk of film speeds, lens settings, multiple exposures, filter systems, strobe flash units, and all the other expensive accessories that can go along with the basic camera equipment.

But you don't have to become a complete shutter nut about buying a camera—the only important thing is that you begin to see and think and feel in camera terms, learn to approach things visually. Because nothing will get you out of abstract theoretical thinking faster than having a camera in your hands and being forced to take the best possible picture of any given subject. All the fancy intellectual thinking vanishes when one has to come to terms with a specific visual image—and then filmmaking and screenwriting become radically practical matters of how to sequence the best possible shots to make an effective moving picture.

And once the screenwriter has a camera in his own hands, he will begin to learn what a peculiar and remarkable instrument the camera really is. He will discover that a camera is almost always remorselessly honest, hideously literal, and ruthlessly truthful. He will find out that even a skilled stage actor cannot fool a camera. The actor may be able to mask over his real feelings onstage in front of a theatre audience, by using a lot of makeup and technical acting tricks—but once that same actor is in front of a camera, he is brought face to face with his own naked emotions, and the camera always sees right through the slightest dishonesty in his facial or physical expression.

Now if it's impossible for a skilled stage actor to fool a camera, how much more impossible it must be for a screenwriter to fake a phony screenplay story line and get away with it in front of a camera! The best actors in the world can't put across a shallow or shoddily conceived filmscript, no matter how hard they may try. Witness any one of a hundred movies that are released each year which may have extraordinarily powerful performances by all of the actors, and yet the screenplay itself is plainly seen as nothing but a desperate crazy quilt covering over a completely implausible story line.

Using a camera can do wonders for a screenwriter's sense of what film work is all about. But what kind of a camera should the screenwriter get? If he can afford it, the ideal unit would be a videocamera with sound, which would enable him to make his own videocassettes for viewing on his home television set. But if a screenwriter doesn't want to make that kind of monetary investment, he can always pick up an inexpensive 8 millimeter or 16 millimeter camera, with a simple screen and projector for viewing of his own movie reels.

And if the screenwriter does not want to get involved in all the footage of taking motion pictures, he can still learn all the important techniques of camera work by getting a 35 millimeter camera to shoot slides, either in black and white or color. Any good camera store will be glad to advise the amateur photographer on the best basic equipment he will need to get started. There is an excellent line of inexpensive and totally automatic 35 millimeter cameras today, complete with automatic loading, focusing, exposure setting, ASA speed sensor, and automatic winding and rewinding. These cameras will run anywhere from $100 to $200.

And if a screenwriter wants to learn more about the actual workings of a camera, he can get a regular 35 millimeter camera base—the most popular makes on the market today are Canon and Minolta and Nikon, but there are also excellent camera bodies made by Pentax, Mamiya, Yashica, Konica, and other American and German manufacturers. This simple 35 millimeter camera body can then be equipped with a whole host of lenses—standard 50 millimeter, 28-100 zoom, 80-200 zoom, 24 and 28 millimeter wide angle lens, fish eye lens for distorted overview, and perhaps a tele-converter that can magnify any of the foregoing lenses two or three times. One can also get a strobe flash attachment for indoor shots, and a variety of lens filters like Skylight or U-V ultraviolet filters for protection from glare. One can choose from a variety of film speeds (ASA 64 to 1600) depending on available light source, although it is usually best to choose one standard speed and then stay with it, so you can learn everything there is to know about how to use that one film speed to best advantage.

This simple 35 millimeter camera equipment—camera body, flash attachment, zoom lens, and teleconverter—should run around $500. Of course you can always acquire more and more accessories, but this basic equipment should be adequate to get the screenwriter into going out and taking his own pictures. And there is really no better way of cultivating a film head than dealing directly with film, for oneself.

Stanley Kubrick tells how he made his first film in 1953

using the most modest equipment imaginable. Kubrick was going to see a lot of films and he became convinced, as he says, "I couldn't make them any worse than the majority of films I was seeing. Bad films gave me the courage to try making a film."[35] So Kubrick raised about $10,000 from a father and an uncle, and he shot his own film with two friends, which was called *Fear and Desire*.

This experience showed Kubrick the extreme simplicity of film work—that a filmmaker does not really need all that much paraphrenalia for the actual making of a movie. "It freed me from any concern again about the technical or logistical aspects of filmmaking." This is an astonishing statement coming from the man who was to go on and make *Paths of Glory*, which is such a tour de force of camera work—extreme mobility of point of view, with the camera moving in, zooming out, and carrying the viewer rapidly along the inside of those first world war trenches past the soldiers who are all huddled up against the sides, and then elevating suddenly upwards over the battlefield itself, with great sweeping panoramic long shots of the night fighting, as phosphorescent flares and rockets illuminate the dismal no man's land.

Kubrick insists it was his beginning work as a filmmaker, his getting out there and using his own camera, that gave him everything he needed to know about motion pictures. And from this early learning to see things in their simplest camera terms, Kubrick went on to make such monuments of technical film achievement as *A Clockwork Orange, Dr. Strangelove,* and the colossal *2001: A Space Odyssey*.

So. The simplest camera work is the beginning of an authentic film head—learning how to frame a shot, and how to see an image from as many different angles as possible, and how to convey a certain mood about an image.

And from there, one can always move on to the more sophisticated uses of photography. For example, you might choose to explore the rapidly changing state of the photographic art, and see how many exciting new innovations are taking place almost daily. You may be interested in learning that there is a Kodak Instagraphic line already on the market that can make instant color 35 mm slides in a quality that is equal to Ektachrome. And you may be amazed to know there is an on-camera accessory such as Lightflex, which reflects light back into the lens and enables a cameraman to modify the film stock in his camera, extending the range of any film from one to three stops. But you don't need to get this involved in photography if you don't choose to—all that really matters is that you stay close to the fundamental thing about film, that it is a physical thing, made up of strips of celluloid or silver nitrate or whatever, on which images appear. And, importantly, any strip of this film can be taken apart and then put back together again, in any number of different sequences and arrangements.

As soon as a screenwriter appreciates these things, the less foggy and idealistic he will be about film, and the more he will come to understand the importance of what film editing is all about.

Editing—the foundation of all film art—the word *montage*, in French, means editing, a putting together, a selective choreography of separate images which are orchestrated together to make up the final film. In Eisenstein's words, montage occurs "when the separate pieces produce, in juxtaposition, the generality, the synthesis of one's theme. This is the image, incorporating the theme."

Of course this aspect of filmmaking is usually left in the hands of a competent film editor, someone who is trained to know just how to juxtapose certain scenes in sequence so they will create a powerful sense of mood or meaning. But it doesn't hurt for the screenwriter to know as much as possible about the underlying principles of film editing because, after all, the screenwriter is the one who will be initiating the entire story line, so it is very much in his own interests to know as much as possible about all the various techniques that go into filmmaking. In that way, the screenwriter can be his own film editor, able to set down certain sequencings of scenes and images that will achieve the effect that he wants, in order to tell the story that he wants to tell.

There are two important principles of how image sequences can be put together on film—collage (which is the juxtaposition of unrelated images), and montage (which is the juxtaposition of related images).

Collage sequences create a sense of chance events and random happenings and accidental occurrences. For example: a shot of two shoes being tossed out a window, is followed by a shot of three people on a speedboat, followed by a shot of a rose petal being torn from a stem. This particular collage sequence of shots may not seem to make much sense to us, but in the context of a film they might highlight a sense of sudden disruption or absurdity that a filmmaker wanted to communicate.

Montage sequences, on the other hand, create a sense of some common theme or pattern of events, or an underlying motif. For example: a shot of leaves falling from a tree, is followed by a shot of bare branches against the sky, followed by a shot of hillsides covered over with autumn leaves. This sequence of shots would probably indicate to us a common theme of autumn and the passage of time.

These two film principles of collage and montage are at work in whatever image arrangements one can possibly make, and they form the basis of all film editing. Any placement or juxtaposition of one image sequence with another image sequence will be either collage or montage.

We can see collage and montage working most clearly in a totally different art form, the classical Japanese haiku poem —that three line, 17 syllable form which dates from the 13th century. A haiku poem will always present a quick series of sharp clear images which are placed next to each other in such a way that they evoke a sudden mood or flash of insight in the reader's mind's eye.

Here is a haiku by one of the first great master haiku poets:

Lonely crow lands
on leafless bough
this autumn evening

Bashō (1644–1694)

One can see that these sharp clear images—the crow, the bough, the autumn evening—evoke a common theme of night falling like a crow on a bough. It is a sudden, haunting, immense experience that we get from this simple haiku, yet the whole power of the poem comes from the simple juxtaposition of images placed next to each other in a particular sequence.

And this embodies the essence of filmic experience because, like the art of film editing, the haiku evokes its strong mood and meaning by the principle of montage.

Now we can make a playful experiment with this haiku —we'll try rearranging the sequence of the images, to see if our rearrangement alters the total effect of the poem. And since there are three separate image elements in the poem, it follows that we can arrange the lines in six different ways, with the Bashō poem itself representing the first possible sequence:

FIRST
SEQUENCE:

Lonely crow lands
on leafless bough
this autumn evening

SECOND
SEQUENCE:

Lonely crow lands
this autumn evening
on leafless bough

THIRD
SEQUENCE:

This autumn evening
lonely crow lands
on leafless bough

FOURTH
SEQUENCE:

This autumn evening
on leafless bough
lonely crow lands

FIFTH
SEQUENCE:

On leafless bough
lonely crow lands
this autumn evening

SIXTH
SEQUENCE:

On leafless bough
this autumn evening
lonely crow lands

We'll leave it to the reader to study the above six sequences and decide what shifts of mood and meaning have taken place in each successive rearrangement. There's no doubt that Bashō's original sequencing is by far the most appropriate, while the other versions provide minor variations of point of view. This much is clear—each separate sequencing represents a slightly different approach to the material, and therefore results in a subtle different experience on the part of the reader.

This playful exercise goes to the heart of film editing, as it demonstrates how images in different sequence can achieve subtly different effects, depending on the order in which the images are arranged.

Now the reader is invited to try making a few playful experiments of his own by rearranging the image sequences in each of the following poems which were all written by great Japanese master haiku poets. In each of these poems, the separate image elements can be set down in six different ways to shift the mood and meaning of the poem experience.

Here are the original haiku poems:

Old pond
frog jumps in
water sound

Bashō (1644–1694)

In Kyō I am
and still I long for Kyō
oh bird of time

Bashō (1644–1694)

Cherry blossoms–right here!
right now!–birds have two legs!
oh horses have four!

Onitsura (1660–1738)

On the great temple bell
settled and sound asleep
a butterfly

Buson (1715–1783)

Dewdrop world
is a dewdrop world
and yet–and yet–

Issa (1762–1826)

Oh snail
climb Mount Fuji
but slowly–slowly–

Issa (1762–1826)

Each of the above poem exercises shows the crucial importance of image sequencing in the techniques of collage and montage. And once a screenwriter masters these simple techniques, he will understand the art of film editing— and will also understand why some film directors fight to retain control over final cut or editing of their films, sometimes insisting that this power be written right into their contracts. Because without total control over the final cut on a film, a director loses control over the appropriate sequencing of the images in the film, and therefore he loses control over the total contour of the finished film itself.

But the screenwriter, like the haiku poet, is the one who is initiating the sequences of all those sharp clear images, so he is the one who must try to train himself to set down the one image sequence which is precisely right, which will create the one mood and meaning that he is after.

We said at the outset of this chapter that it was important

for a screenwriter to develop a film head—by seeing paintings and photographs, and by seeing as many movies as possible, and also by trying to get himself involved in the filmmaking process by getting a camera and shooting pictures himself, to train himself to think and feel and see in purely visual terms. And we even suggested that a screenwriter should learn as much as possible about the editing techniques which are such a crucial part of filmmaking.

A screenwriter is always better off if he has a film head, which means having a sharp eye for the right image in its most appropriate sequence.

Six

THE PROCESS OF WRITING · PAGE BY
PAGE AND DAY BY DAY · FILM SCHOOLS?

Now comes the chips down, brass tacks challenge when the screenwriter finally faces the naked page of his own screenplay, and the deadline of trying to achieve a certain word count every day, and the no-nonsense ordeal of the screenwriter's endlessly trying to rewrite his own writing.

And beyond all this mechanical difficulty, there is the further terror of the screenwriter's trying to get himself into a trance state writing process so he can learn to trust his own instincts as he keeps himself in the ongoing momentum of writing, writing, writing.

Inertia?—what should a writer do about his resistance to getting the whole thing started, and his continual excuses for why he can't begin on it today, and all the petty errands he suddenly remembers that he should be doing, just as he's about to get down to the real business of writing?

Blocks?—what should a writer do about all those dry periods, pencil sharpenings, ashtray emptyings, long distance phone calls to faraway friends, or going out for long walks alone late at night?

Self-doubt?—how can a writer deal with all those frightening demon furies which may be unleashed out of his own unconscious, to haunt and harrass him while he is trying his damndest to concentrate on the job at hand?

There simply are no rules for how a writer should get into the experience of his own writing, except to say the most obvious thing imaginable—that a writer writes. It is what a writer does, no more, no less. And if a writer wants to write badly enough, then he will damn well overcome all the inertia and blocks and self-doubt that always tend to keep the writer from his own writing.

Beyond that, there are no rules. Some writers write best when they write on a regular schedule, other writers write best if they can stay up all night, other writers write best when they are on marathon spurts of endless energy, and other writers write best if they plan everything out carefully in their heads before they begin to write anything down.

There aren't any rules. And as for the actual act of writing itself, some writers write it all out in longhand first, while other writers prefer to write directly onto the typewriter or use word processors so they can arrange their words and phrases before they commit anything to print.

No rules. One simply has to do it the way one has to do it. And that means having some elementary self-knowing and understanding of one's own peculiar metabolism so one can know what will work best for oneself.

But while we can say that there are no rules for how a writer should go about trying to write his own writing, we can certainly say one or two things about how a writer might try to get himself into the right state of mind so he can begin on his own writing. One thing that is important for each individual writer is trying to reach a degree of inner relaxation and an openness to his own imagination, no matter what peculiar living forms it may happen to take.

Ingmar Bergman expresses this well:

The best time in the writing, I think, is the time when I have no ideas about how to do it. I can lie down on the sofa and I can look into the fire and I can go to the seaside and I can just sit down and do nothing. I just play the game, you know, and it's wonderful and I make some notes and I can go on for a year. Then, when I have made the plan, the difficult job starts: I have to sit down on my ass every morning at ten o'clock and write the screenplay. And then something very, very strange happens: often the personalities in my scripts don't want the same thing I want. If I try to force them to do what I want them to do, it will always be an artistic catastrophe. But if I let them free to do what they want and what they tell me, it's OK.[36]

Another writer, Leo Connellan, describes the process of trying to reach a degree of inner relaxation:

I have to lie down for long periods at a time—I seem to be out of it completely, no good for anything—but then I get this incredible energy, and I don't know where it comes from . . .[37]

Of course, this experience can be very frightening—to suspend oneself so completely, and trust that one will tap into some unknown energy system—it feels like the psyche is going on a space walk, with no external support systems to hold onto.

This trying to reach a degree of inner relaxation has something to do with turning one's critical mind off, not unlike what happens when a patient lies down on a couch in an analyst's office and begins saying the first thing that comes into his mind.

And in fact it was Sigmund Freud who wrote the best description of this process of trying to achieve an inner relaxation, in the opening pages of his book *The Interpretation of Dreams* (1900). We can summarize what Freud says there in our own rough paraphrase:

Freud speaks of "a certain psychic preparation" that is necessary to interprete dreams . . . first, to eliminate the critical spirit in which someone is ordinarily in the

83

habit of viewing his thoughts . . . to do this, one has to take up a restful position and close his eyes . . . renounce all criticism of the thought-formations which he may perceive to be going on inside his mind . . . also noting and communicating everything that comes to his attention, he must not allow himself to suppress any idea because it may seem unimportant or irrelevant or nonsensical . . . he must preserve an absolute impartiality in respect to his ideas . . . Freud calls this process "self-observation" where an unlimited number of thoughts will enter one's consciousness which would otherwise have eluded his grasp . . . "The point is to induce a psychic state which is in some degree analogous, as regards the distribution of psychic energy (mobile attention), to the state of mind before falling asleep—and also, of course, to the hypnotic state." . . . Freud quotes the German poet Schiller (1788) who says that in creative work, one has to guard against any constraint which the intellect may impose on the imagination . . . which is to say, he must withdraw "the watchers from the gates," in order to allow anything to come in that may want to . . .[38]

As we said, all this may sound very simple and very easy, but it can be terrifying to someone who is not in the habit of relaxing his critical thought processes. Besides, how dare anyone waste so much time lying down on a couch, and letting his thoughts wander, when he should be up and working? The whole civilization seems to be set against anyone who may appear to be such a loafer, not doing any immediately apparent useful work, but only trying to observe his own creative mental processes.

Still, it's not so hard to turn one's back on all those superficial pressures, and try to master the technique of entering into a state of inner relaxation. And then one can begin to observe the pure flow of visual images that are taking place inside one's head—as if one were simply watching a film that is being shown in one's own mind, continuously. And because one relinquishes control over all of one's critical thoughts, it will be like watching a movie where one does not really know the outcome.

This is one approach to getting into the process of one's own screenwriting—learning to dip into one's own unconscious, perhaps even do a little deep sea diving inside oneself, to see what one will come up with.

There is another approach that does not depend so much on freeing one's own unconscious imagery—there may already be so much going on in the contemporary everyday consciousness of the writer that he does not need to get anything out of himself. Political and social events may be so drastic and radical that the screenwriter may want to work them right into a screenplay, either directly or in a disguised form.

Carl Foreman reports using this approach in the writing of *High Noon* (1952), the classic western that starred Gary Cooper and Grace Kelly:

I started to do *High Noon* back in 1949 when the UnAmerican Activities Committee was just going into high gear in its Hollywood investigations—so-called —and I could see this community beginning to crumble around the edges as these high-powered politicians came in accompanied by the headlines they were getting in the local press, and so forth, and putting this community through an inquisition that was getting more and more painful all the time for a lot of people, and people were falling by the wayside one way or another. They were either capitulating to these gangsters . . . political gangsters from out of town, or they were being executed by them and by the people who worked with them here. And I could see that my time was coming sooner or later . . . it was just being delayed a couple of years or so . . . and I wanted to write about that. I wanted to write about what I considered the death of Hollywood. So that all shaped the writing of *High Noon*. That was very conscious, see.

And that, incidentally, was a story of fear, because this was a community that was terribly afraid at that time, and there was . . . you could almost smell the fear that rose, it was like the smog that we have now, you could see it.[39]

So then one has a choice of two basic approaches to writing any original screenplay—one can either try to tap into the images in one's own unconscious, or one can get at it quite consciously, using the raw stuff of contemporary events that may be taking place all around one.

Of course there will also be a whole host of historical and biographical and fictional materials that one has at one's disposal as well, to draw on in the writing of any original screenplay. But how one goes about using any of these materials will inevitably engage either the unconscious or the conscious processes that we have been discussing.

There isn't much to be said, one way or the other, as to which approach is better—the unconscious or the conscious. It depends on the individual screenwriter and whether he thinks he will work more truly and more movingly using an unconscious or a conscious approach to his materials. And if he's not sure, he can always try experimenting with either approach until he can locate his own unique relationship to the material that is inside or outside of him.

As for the actual mechanics of writing, of course it's an individual matter that one has to work out for oneself. However, one could probably learn a great deal from William Goldman's excellent advice:

I think screenplays should be written with as much speed as possible—and with even more deliberation. By "as much speed as possible" I don't mean to suggest you should throw a bag over its head and do it for Old Glory. But I do believe that you should push yourself hard and continually. What's important to decide here is your own specific pace. If, for example, when you're going well, you do one to two pages a day when you write a screenplay, I would try and reach the second number. If you do seven to ten when you're rolling, try and get to ten. The reasoning (if you can call it that) is, I believe somehow that extra energy translates itself to the page, and from there to the reader. Maybe it does, anyway. Maybe sometimes.[40]

There are many special techniques that a screenwriter can use in scripting his own original screenplay. One special technique is the use of comic strips, which always jump from one image-picture to another. The screenwriter might try to set up his own comic strip, to represent how certain film shots will jump to certain other film shots.

Another special technique is the use of 3 x 5 cards to build a screenplay format. The screenwriter can try laying out certain scenes on various 3 x 5 cards, and then he will be free to shuffle the scenes around and rearrange them into new sequences.

These special techniques—using comic strips and 3 x 5 cards—have proven useful for some screenwriters. However, in all fairness, we should say that some other filmmakers object violently to these methods. One veteran filmmaker, Carl Foreman, is particularly bothered by the use of 3 x 5 cards:

I'm always surprised by writers who tell me how they put things on filing cards, you see? And sometimes they spread them out, or they deal them out like a deck of cards, and they find they can take a card scene here and put it there and so forth and so on. That intrigues me very much and I'm impressed by that—some of them are quite good writers. Well, I don't work that way. It seems to me incredible that you can take a scene that by any process of judgment has to go at a certain time, a certain place in the development of the characters . . . the development of the story . . . and place it some-place else . . . staggers me . . . Unless you're doing a flashback . . . Unless it's part of a technical bit of

jugglery-pokery you're doing. So I don't do that . . .
I'm not saying it's wrong, I just wouldn't know how to
do that.[41]

As for the matter of rewriting, of course one will always
have to go back over everything one has written, and one
will have to try to apply the most strenuous kind of self-
editing imaginable. Here again, there are no rules—except
the simplest rule, which is that one will always have to
measure what one has written against the remorseless
standard of what it was that one really wanted to write. And
often this may lead a screenwriter into the very highest kind
of sacrificial art—he may find himself faced with the necessity of cutting whole sections from his work which he thought
were his finest work. And these sections might not be such
writing in themselves, in fact they might be excellent
sections—but they just don't happen to belong in this
particular screenplay that he is trying to write. That can be a
very painful exercise of honesty. But William Faulkner once
said, "You must learn to kill all your darlings." What he
meant by that was, you must be ready to throw out what you
thought were your dandiest ideas and your niftiest lines if
they do not really fit with the context of what you are trying
to create.

All this discussion of the process of screenwriting leads us
inevitably to the question: what about film schools? Would it
be worth it for the screenwriter to enroll in any of the film
departments at any one of the leading universities, to receive
expert technical guidance which he simply can't pick up on
his own?

There are different points of view about this, and all we
can do here is set down a few of the opinions and let the
reader decide for himself.

One view from a top film studio executive, is that film
schools are not all that important for the screenwriter:

I don't want to be negative about them, but I don't
really feel it's essential to go to film school to write a

good screenplay at all. I think you have to have a film head. I think you have to be very much aware that a film is visual, it's action, it tells a story—you have to be a lover of film, you have to be well versed, you have to have many many hours watching it—that doesn't mean you have to be a film buff, and know who starred in what films in 1936. But you do have to understand what a feature film really is.[42]

Another view, from someone who is currently teaching advanced courses in screenwriting at one of the leading universities, is that film schools can be extremely useful to the young screenwriter:

Writing is a learnable art . . . and a good screenwriting course can be very helpful if only to focus on where someone writes, and how someone writes, and when someone writes—and who one imagines as one's audience . . . Instead of writing "he came downstairs feeling bad," the young screenwriter can be trained to write "he came downstairs tearing at his beard"—in other words, translating the mood into a visual image . . . And you can go on and train the young screenwriter to construct his whole picture silently, without any dialogue, so he will have to stay as close as possible to the living image.[43]

If one does want to investigate good film schools in the United States, there are four major universities at the present time which offer advanced degrees in screenwriting. On the West Coast, the University of California at Los Angeles (UCLA) and the University of Southern California (USC) offer courses in filmmaking and screenwriting, and both departments offer B.F.A. and M.F.A. degrees in these fields. On the East Coast, Columbia University and New York University are the two major universities offering similar degrees in filmmaking and screenwriting.

One of these universities, N.Y.U., has an Institute of Film

and Television at the Tisch School of the Arts at Washington Square, New York City, where there are some 1100 undergraduates enrolled in the program, and some 30 graduate students. The course offerings in cinema studies include such classes as the following:

"The Craft of Visual and Dramatic Writing"
"Playwriting (Beginning and Advanced)"
"Screenwriting (Beginning and Advanced)"
"Developing the Screenplay"
"Comedy Workshop"
"Fiction Writing"
"Text Analysis—Plays"
"Text Analysis—Film Scripts"

The current N.Y.U. Institute faculty includes Ring Lardner Jr., Tad Mosel, Venable Herndon, Ian Hunter, Waldo Salt, and other professionals who have earned their credentials in the film industry.

In addition to the universities which offer formal study programs in filmmaking, there are several less academic service organizations which offer programs for the screenwriter.

One such organization is The American Film Institute, established in 1967 by the National Endowment for the Arts, with this mailing address:

THE AMERICAN FILM INSTITUTE

The John F. Kennedy Center for the Performing Arts
Washington, D. C. 20566

The Institute's stated purpose is to advance the motion picture as an art form, and it seeks to preserve important film and video materials, and also develop new talent. Members of the American Film Institute regularly receive *American Film* magazine, and the *Close-Up* newsletter, as well as discount admissions to films in Washington, Los Angeles, and London. Members also receive admission to special seminars and lectures and other events at the American Film Institute in Washington. The Institute also organizes touring film programs such as "New Arab Cinema," "New Films from East Germany," "China Film Work," etc.

Another service organization is the Center for Advanced Film Studies, founded in 1969 in Los Angeles, where regular seminars are held, and where there are workshop programs to teach the basic filmmaking craft.

But whether one chooses to make use of any of these professional service organizations, or whether one chooses to enroll at any of the more formal filmmaking programs at any of the leading universities, or whether one chooses to go it alone—this much will always be true: the actual process of trying to write one's own original screenplay, page by page and day by day, will always entail considerable personal discipline, a lot of false starts and a lot of inevitable revisions, and it will also require the kind of fierce determination which has to characterize any artist pursuing any particular art form.

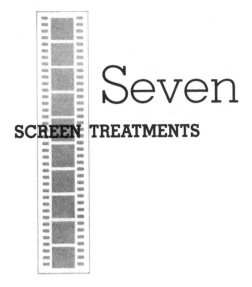

Seven

SCREEN TREATMENTS

A screenplay treatment will be a synopsis of the principal events of the story line of a proposed film script—it will be a resumé of the outstanding visuals, a rundown of the characters, and a description of the crucial moments of the script. A screenplay treatment should also try to state the theme or motif of the story line in a single sentence, in as simple and as compelling a way as possible. Also, the screenplay treatment will almost always be written in the present tense, to give it more reality and immediacy.

One should always remember that a screenplay treatment is usually written to interest an agent or a producer or a director in taking on the proposed project, and so the screenwriter should try to make each treatment as exciting and effective as possible.

In Europe, a screenplay treatment is usually called an *exposée*, and it will consist of two or three pages of the simple story line—no dialogue, no narrative, just pure exposition of what happens. But in America, it is usually the custom to include much more than this in a treatment—there will not only be a summary of the basic story line, but also some sample dialogue, and some indication of the narrative flow, some characterization, and the highlights or key moments in the film.

This screenplay treatment format can run anywhere from 5 to 75 pages, depending on how extensive it has to be.

Just as there are as many different kinds of screenplays as there are different kinds of films, so there will be as many different kinds of treatments as there are different kinds of screenplays. The essential characteristic of the treatment will always be the same, which is to present some clear idea of what the final screenplay version will be like.

There are generally three different types of screenplay treatment formats which a screenwriter may wish to execute:

1. An original free-lance screenplay treatment. This will come out of an author's own imagination, and it will be his own story line and his own characters and he will develop the entire scenario by himself, in screenplay treatment form, hoping to interest an agent or a producer in commissioning him to execute the complete screenplay filmscript. He will, of course, be offering this free-lance treatment to the open market, with no guarantee that it will be picked up and purchased by a film producer.

2. A screenplay treatment "on spec" or speculation. This will usually come out of a producer's imagination, he will have some idea of something he thinks he would like to film, and he will give this idea to the screenwriter and ask him to develop it in treatment form, to see how the screenwriter would handle it. But the producer will retain the option of turning down the treatment if it is not the way he wants it. In this case, the screenwriter is also writing on risk with no guarantee of a sale, although here he will at least know that the idea already appeals to the film producer.

3. A screenplay treatment for a format film or TV program. This will be a treatment for a particular film series or

television program series where the ongoing themes and characters are already fixed, and the screenwriter must adapt his story line to the context of the ongoing series format, using the same style and characters and not altering them appreciably in the screenplay treatment.

Of course there will be some aspects of preparing screenplay treatments that may make a screenwriter feel that he is, indeed, a "writer for hire." Worse than that, he may sometimes feel like a studio hack, a lackie, someone who is being paid to execute someone else's ideas, and that may inspire resentment sometimes.

Nor is it only the beginning screenwriter who may feel this way. Eleanor Perry, the author of *David and Lisa* and *The Swimmer* and *Diary of a Mad Housewife*, speaks for many professional screenwriters when she voices her impatience with the writing of screenplay treatments:

> The last thing I want to start with is a treatment, which is a big Hollywood thing . . . a treatment being a kind of synopsis in the present tense. I loathe it, and I have refused now. I never would write another treatment as long as I live . . .[44]

Of course this is one of our outstanding screenwriters speaking, and perhaps she has earned the right to vow never to write another treatment. And perhaps she will be able to hold to that promise because of the success of her own past work. But screenwriters with lesser credentials than Eleanor Perry had better reconcile themselves to writing screenplay treatments as an inevitable part of the film industry.

Even so, writing treatments may seem too much like writing term papers or doing book reports in high school —those dry, lifeless contraptions that one had to hack out on demand just to prove one knew what one was doing. One winces at the memory of all night typing and trying to psyche out a particular teacher in order to get what one wants. And to be sure, every screenplay treatment is a poor

95

substitute for the full-length screenplay which one really wants to write, and it is, God knows, a far cry from the finished full-length feature film itself. But if one wants to be a screenwriter badly enough, one should be able to overcome all these psychological obstacles to turning out a first-rate screenplay treatment.

While we're on the subject, however, there is one other unpleasant fact to be faced about writing screenplay treatments. It's obvious that out of the tremendous number of treatments that are written, only a very small percentage of them will ever be picked up and taken into execution as full-length feature films. And the reason for this is also obvious—there are so many people out there who want to have a hand in writing films. The Library of Congress receives about 20,000 screenplays a year to copyright, but the major studios only produce about 150 films a year, and the independent filmmakers only account for a few hundred more films each year. So the competition to sell screenplays and treatments is not only fierce, it can reach insane proportions. And the writer has to know this as he begins work on his treatment—because it's all the more reason to make it exceptionally good, the best of its kind, so it will stand a chance in the marketplace.

One screenwriter we spoke with told us that out of over 100 treatments he had written in his lifetime, only about 5% of them had ever been picked up and taken into production. But when one thinks of what it can mean to have five full-length feature films to one's credit, the other 95 treatments don't seem like such a waste after all.

A treatment, then, is a legitimate part of the film industry and one should know how to execute it according to certain standard guidelines.

Here is how Rosanne Ehrlich, Literary Director of Paramount Pictures, describes the format of the typical screenplay treatment:

A treatment can be from 4 or 5 pages, to 70 pages—that is an outline, which is just a drawing of the structure of the screenplay. A treatment usually tends to have more of characterization, perhaps a little dialogue, something about the relationship between the characters. It certainly outlines the plot, and it gives you a sense of mood, and hopefully it gives you a sense of the visual also. So a treatment is a more tangible feeling about what the film will be.[45]

We also said a good screenplay treatment should try to state the theme or motif of the story line in a single sentence, in as simple and compelling a way as possible. To sharpen this skill, it's an interesting exercise to try summing up the central theme or motif of a film that one has already seen.

Here is an example of a one sentence summary of the theme of the 1940 John Ford film, *The Grapes of Wrath*, based on the John Steinbeck novel. We'll try to give some idea of what the whole story is all about:

This American epic is the chronicle of a family of migratory farm workers in its struggle to survive after it was dispossessed by the upheaval of the Great Depression, and how this family had to eke out an existence in its quest for dignity and gainful employment.

This is a fair statement of the theme of *The Grapes of Wrath*, but it sounds a bit too bookish and sociological—if we read this kind of plot summary in the TV listing of our local papers, it probably wouldn't strike us as the kind of film we'd care to spend two hours watching tonight. Yet we know *The Grapes of Wrath* is one of the most powerful and compelling films ever made, so where have we failed to capture this excitement in our summary of the film story?

Well, for one thing, the diction of that one sentence summary is so impossibly erudite, and the word choices are so pretentious, that they throw up a fog around the real drama of the story and make it sound more like a book report or a term paper than a living story about real human beings.

And that's not the sort of thing that would really excite an agent or a producer. So let's try it again, and see if we can't make the film story come more alive:

This is the story of the Joads from Oklahoma—Ma, Pa, Tom, Rose O'Sharon, Grandpa and Grandma—and how they all have to leave their land, pack their belongings on a rickety used car, and drift from one makeshift shanty town to another, looking for an honest day's pay and a little fair play as they make their way out to the promised land of California.

That's a little better—perhaps because we were able to cut down on all those generalities and get in a few more specific image details. Place names help, and so do proper names. Notice also we put the whole thing in the present tense, which gives it more reality and immediacy. Also, we chucked all those ten dollar Latinate words and tried to use as many plain style monosyllable Anglo-Saxon words as possible.

Writing this kind of summary statement of a theme isn't easy, and one has to keep tinkering with it to create a sentence that will be both accurate and compelling. But once one masters this simple exercise, one has gone a long way towards mastering the skill of turning out a persuasive screenplay treatment.

Here are a few more examples of summary statements, based on films that have already been made. The first is *Paths of Glory*, the 1957 film by Stanley Kubrick:

In the first World War, three French soldiers are chosen at random to face a kangaroo court martial and execution in front of a firing squad, as an example to their division after it fails to achieve an impossible military objective while fighting in Verdun.

And here is another summary statement, based on the 1961 Stanley Kramer film of *Judgment at Nuremberg*:

Behind the scenes at the Nazi war crimes trials in Germany, all the individual story lines raise the question of whether anyone can ever be held accountable for carrying out the orders of a superior officer, no matter how sick and twisted those orders may be.

As we said, it isn't always easy, and one could keep on tinkering with these statements to get in more specific image details and more place names and proper names. One should try doing it with the last three or four or five films that one has seen, to get the knack of writing simple summary statements that are both simple and compelling. Hopefully, this knack will carry over into the actual writing of the screenplay treatment as well. And of course the real skill will be writing something that will excite someone else enough to want to buy it.

Here is an example of a screenplay treatment in the form of a simple synopsis of the story line. It is taken from a studio campaign book which is trying to promote a finished film, and so there is not much emphasis on visuals, or on real character development, or on the execution of the actual screenplay script. It is a simple overview, and as such it gives the idea of what the story line itself is all about.

A synopsis treatment of this sort is extremely valuable to show the story line, but it is not necessarily written to sell the screenplay, nor is it interested in exciting a producer so he will buy the treatment. It is just a simple narrative account of what happens in the story line.

The treatment is for the film *Giant*, starring James Dean and Rock Hudson and Elizabeth Taylor and Mercedes McCambridge. The screenwriters on this film were Fred Guiol and Ivan Moffat, who were hired to adapt Edna Ferber's 447 page novel set in Texas. The screenwriters were able to condense the novel into a 178 page script.

Bick Benedict (Rock Hudson), the young owner of a half-million-acre cattle ranch in Texas, comes to Maryland to buy a magnificent black stallion. He meets, falls in love with and quickly marries Leslie (Elizabeth Taylor). Though they are much in love, there are many clashes of temperament at their vast Reate Ranch, so different from Leslie's home in Maryland. Leslie is shocked at the status of the Mexican ranch hands who are underpaid and underprivileged. She takes matters into her own hands by giving them medical care. A stubborn spinster, Bick's sister, Luz (Mercedes McCambridge), runs the house. Her unreasonable rule over the Reata Ranch is ended when she is killed in a fall while riding. In her will, she leaves a small piece of her land to Jett Rink (James Dean), a violent young ranch hand who continuously quarrels with Bick while dreaming of the day he will make his own million. He is convinced that his new property is the beginning of his fortune and his dreams will soon come true. He strikes oil and goes on to great riches. Leslie and Bick have three children who, when grown up, all go against the wishes of their parents. Their son, Jordy, announces his marriage to Juana, a beautiful Mexican girl who is studying medicine. Bick is dismayed at the idea of having a Mexican girl as Mrs. Jordan Benedict III. Reluctantly, all the Benedicts accept an invitation to the elaborate opening of the new hotel owned by the now fabulously wealthy Jett Rink. Bick is furious to discover his daughter Luz as Queen of Jett's spectacular model parade. When Juana is refused service in the beauty salon of the hotel, an enraged Jordy looks for Jett, whom he considers responsible for the insult to his wife. He finds him in the banquet room as Jett is about to deliver his dedication speech. Before Jordy can land a punch, two henchmen pin his arms back while Jett knocks him out. Bick then challenges Jett to a fight outside, but Jett is so drunk and helpless that Bick leaves him in disgust. Later, Jett passes out cold on the speaker's dias before he can deliver his speech. Young Luz is angry at Jordan for the way she thinks they have disgraced the family and ruined Jett's big evening and goes to the darkened banquet room where the still drunk Jett is delivering his speech to an empty room. Completely disillusioned, Luz returns to her parents. Bick and his family drive to Reata. In a mood of relief and good cheer, they stop by a diner on the highway. A burly young man eyes Luz with distaste, and shortly afterwards orders some impoverished Mexican travellers out. Bick fights him but is no match for the much younger man and ends up on the floor. Back at Reata, Bick grumbles to Leslie that he has been a failure, that nothing has worked out as he planned it. In Leslie's eyes, Bick was at last fighting for fundamental justice and she yells at him: "After a hundred years, the Benedict family is a real big success."[46]

As we said, this treatment is a simple synopsis of the story line, and it does not try to present any visuals or any real description of the characters or any highlights of the crucial moments in the film. Nor is there any summary statement of the theme or motif of the film. It is, quite simply, a quick sketch of the story line, very like those plot summaries of soap operas you see printed in local daily papers to condense the basic happenings of the ongoing serial.

Now if a screenwriter really wanted to capture the imagination of an agent or a producer, he would have to build on this simple kind of synopsis story line. He would have to describe some of the outstanding visuals of the film—what it looked like when the oil rigging suddenly began to explode with black gold all over the faces of the men who were standing by, awestruck by the oil gush. And he might want to put in some of the dialogue, to give a sample of what the characters really sound like. And he might want to dwell on some of the important moments in the film, to give some idea of what the finished film will feel like.

Here is another screenplay treatment, this one a little more fleshed out. It is obviously written with the intention of interesting an agent or a producer in commissioning it.

It is an original free-lance screenplay treatment entitled

First Father, and it is an outline for a full-length feature film. First we will print the treatment showing the appropriate screenplay treatment format as it was set down by the author, and then we will identify the piece and describe what happened to this treatment as it made its way through the film industry.

First there is a title page, with the proposed title "FIRST FATHER" all in capitals, followed by a sub-title: "Outline for a film." Then there is the author's full name, his telephone number, and mailing address. There may be a copyright notice also if the author so desires.

Then there is the following screenplay treatment:

Tom Grove, 37, an M.D., gets an appointment as resident physician at a co-educational prep school in Darby, a small town on the Housatonic River in western Connecticut. The school, a mix of Collegiate Gothic and Colonial clapboard, is just across a covered bridge from town, and only half an hour's drive up Route 7 from New Milford, where Tom grew up. After his recent divorce, from an ambitious pre-occupied labor lawyer with whom he has had no children, and disastrous financial battles with a crew of money-grubbing doctors and dentists with whom he tried partnership in a Dobbs Ferry medical complex, Tom is glad to get away to the quiet of the countryside, especially to the brooks and meadows and mountains of the Housatonic Valley which he has loved since childhood. His office windows look out across the river at a broad sweep of corn fields, and beyond to gentle mountains covered with green all the way to the top.

Tom's contract with Darby School allows him to develop a town practice so long as it doesn't interfere with the service he provides students, staff, and faculty. One Saturday afternoon, when the town's Main Street doctor is off boating, a day student, Ann Keeler, 14, is brought to Tom's office suffering from an ankle broken in a field hockey accident. While Tom is treating the girl he gets the impression that he knows her, but quickly ascribes this feeling to the probability that he has seen her before, if not on the school grounds, then on the town green, in the drugstore, or at the post office.

Living in a school-owned and serviced cottage, and eating in the school dining hall, Tom is constantly surrounded by people, and yet he is lonely. There is no one who really knows who he is—that kind of relationship takes a while to develop. Of course the headmaster, Arnold Robertson, and his wife, Dorothy, are cordial, and there are lots of attractive, intelligent teachers and students to talk to, and play tennis with, but all this is far from the intimacy that Tom longs for, and now realizes that he didn't have with either his ex-wife, or with any of the men he worked with or near at the medical complex. And as the weeks pass, Tom begins to see that he is in an odd position. He's not exactly a faculty member, and certainly not a student, and not a townie, either. Except for occasional bouts of gossip with his nurse, Mrs. Beacomb, a large, pleasant, red-haired woman, the wife of the resident state policeman, he is in limbo.

Tom makes an effort to get to be better friends with the headmaster, and one evening, sitting last at the faculty table over brandy in the headmaster's semi-enclosed dining alcove, Tom looks out across the large dining room at a table of fourth-form girls, laughing and arguing after dinner. He is suddenly reminded of Ann Keeler, and he tells Arnold about her, and how he has been bothered by her resemblance to someone—he doesn't know who, and even as he is saying this he realizes that the girl reminds him of the woman with whom he had a relationship before going to Viet-Nam. He has another brandy and tells Arnold about the affair; how Sally Fowler, that was her name, got pregnant only a few weeks before he was scheduled to fly off, how they both agreed that it would be better for her to have an abortion rather than raise a fatherless child. Tom knew that he had only a fair chance of returning from the war, and felt particularly strongly about being around to raise his kid because his own father walked out on him and his mother when he was six. He and Sally had even agreed to split the abortion expenses to show their accord in the matter. He'd given her his half in cash on the night before reporting for duty. Robertson nods sympathetically, and then excuses himself to correct a batch of papers he's gotten from his honors history class.

That evening, Tom drinks more brandy in his cottage, and goes to bed thinking about Sally. Just before dawn he wakes up from a dream in which he has seen Sally and Ann standing together in white dresses. He fumbles about in a still unpacked suitcase and pulls out a photo album in which he turns to a picture of his mother and her sister at a high school graduation. He discovers that Ann also looks like his mother's sister.

Next morning he takes the picture to his office, and when Ann returns for treatment of her ankle, he puts the photo in an open desk drawer so he can compare Ann to his aunt. He finds that he is not just imagining things. Ann does look like Aunt Julia, and if his memory holds, she also looks like Sally Fowler—he has not seen Sally for at least 14 years. He wonders where she is, and what she is doing. Probably married with several kids. She had wanted to be a swimming coach, but was having a hard time finding a job.

When the office closes Tom asks Mrs. Beacomb about Ann and says that she looks a lot like people he used to know. Mrs. Beacomb says that Ann comes from an old Darby family—the Keelers helped found Darby, she thinks—and that Ann lives on a big farm up on Cobble Road. Her father owns half the town—he's in real estate and insurance, and her mother raises Morgan horses, and has more money than the father. "They've got everything," says Mrs. Beacomb, "except . . . except."

Tom presses her. "Except they couldn't have kids. Ann is adopted."

Haunted by Ann's face, Tom says he is going to take a few day's vacation on Cape Cod, but when he reaches Hartford he takes a motel room and begins to make the rounds of the state vital statistics offices and the adoption and welfare agencies. He says that he has an adopted patient, Ann Keeler, and that he suspects by certain symptoms that she may be suffering from an inherited inability to digest lactose, but he must find out her true family medical history if he is to treat her successfully. Finally he manages to wine and dine a sympathetic clerk into "borrowing" Ann's adoption certificate from the files long enough for him to take down the name of her real mother. Barely able to conceal his shock, he sees that Ann's mother's name is Sally Fowler—the name of the woman with whom he was having a relationship before leaving for Viet-Nam. She didn't have the abortion after all. She had the baby and gave it away. Masking his emotion as best he can, he thanks the official, and returns to Darby.

For days after his return he is so distracted that he can hardly fulfill his medical duties. And Mrs. Beacomb, who notices that he is getting nervous and run-down, urges him to take a longer vacation before the fall term starts and makes it impossible to get away. Ann and her mother have taken a liking to Dr. Grove, and during a final visit in which he removes Ann's bandages and declares the ankle pretty well healed, Ann's mother invites him for dinner on Saturday night. He nervously refuses, and then accepts. Ann's father takes a liking to Tom, and soon he has become a family friend, dining frequently at Ann's house, and even going on family outings like the traditional July 4th picnic at Lake Waramaug. Tom and Ann go rowing on the lake, and as they are coming in, just at twilight, Ann asks Tom if a lot of the kids he treats at school are adopted. Tom says that quite a few seem to be, yes, but why does she ask? She confesses that she is adopted and wants desperately to find her natural mother, but doesn't want to offend her adopted family. Once she brought the subject up while her mother was slicing vegetables, and her mother raised the slicing knife and said she'd kill anyone who tried to take Ann away from her. But Ann wonders if Tom, whom she has come to like and trust, wouldn't help her try to find her real mother. Tom wants with all his heart to tell her right then and there that he is her real father, but he doesn't dare for fear of the shock she will feel, and the shock that her parents, who have become his friends, will experience. He agrees to help Ann, although he doesn't know what success he will have because her mother has probably, he tells Ann, gotten married by now and taken her husband's name so it will be hard to find her under her original name, even if he succeeds in discovering what that is. He explains that the laws sealing adoption records are usually strict.

Tom becomes so disturbed by all this that he takes the headmaster into his confidence, and the older man advises him, if he can stand it, to let sleeping dogs lie, and wait until the girl grows up and away from her family a bit more. But Tom can't stand it, and he begins searching for Sally Fowler, combing phone books and hospital records and eventually tracking down Sally's widowed mother, who tells him that Sally has indeed married, and then divorced—"a terrible shame," and is living with her son in Danbury, where she has gotten a job as a swimming coach, the work she had always wanted, and finally been able to do after all these years.

Tom goes to see Sally at her high school, and finds her, after team practice, by the pool. She is stunned to see him, but soon calms down and confesses that she simply couldn't bring herself to abort the baby, but had no way of supporting her either because she couldn't tell her family, strict Catholics, what had happened.

Tom tells her how he found Ann, and that the child is looking for her mother, but dares not offend her adoptive parents whom she loves very much, and who love her with a protective passion. Sally invites Tom to dinner and he meets her son, Jack. They part, promising to keep in touch, not knowing what they are going to do about their daughter Ann.

A few days later, when Mrs. Keeler invites Tom to dinner, she asks him why he doesn't sometime bring a date. When he hangs up, Tom calls Sally, and proposes a plan. She will come to dinner as his date and get a chance to see their daughter. She says she will think it over, and seems at first to be refusing, but calls back late that same night to accept. Tom wonders if he should somehow take Ann into his confidence, but decides that she will not be able to handle it, and waits to see if she will like Sally.

The dinner goes off well. Afterwards, in the car, Sally breaks down and cries as Tom drives her home to Danbury. Tom proposes that he tell Ann, when the time seems right, that she has seen her mother, and says that he might have a chance of taking Ann on an afternoon outing so that Sally and Ann can meet again.

When Ann comes for annual pre-school physical in early September, Tom tells her that she has met her mother, and asks her if she wants to see her again. Ann remembers the dinner and begins to cry, but soon gets hold of herself and she and Tom work out a plan. She will ask her parents if Tom and his "girlfriend" can take her to the Agricultural Fair at Bridgewater.

The parents agree. And when the day comes, Tom calls Ann up and drives her to Danbury, where they pick up Sally and her son, Jack, and drive to the fair. Tom gets Jack involved in shooting for prizes so that Sally and Ann can have some time together alone. Mother and daughter buy a huge ball of cotton candy, get sticky eating it, embrace, cry, embrace again, and then Ann asks Sally timidly if she knows who her father

107

is. Sally hesitates and then points across the fair ground at Tom. Ann is surprised, pleased, stunned, and wants to know why he hasn't told her earlier. Sally explains that he was terrified of hurting her, and would never have intruded on her life at all if "you hadn't asked him to help you find me."

When Sally and Ann come back Tom can see from the way Ann is looking at him that she knows he is her father. He breaks into tears, and Jack wants to know why a big man like Tom is crying, and Sally says she will explain it all later. Tom hugs Ann, and everybody but Jack starts to cry. Ann puts her arm on Jack's shoulder and tells him that she is his half-sister, and Jack runs off, confused and hurt. When they find Jack again and head for home, calm has returned. In the car, before she gets out at her house in Darby, Ann tells Tom that she has decided to wait a while before she tells her adoptive parents, and Tom agrees that this is a good idea. He promises to bring Sally to dinner from time to time. "She's nice," says Ann, "I can see why you like her." "Yes," says Tom, "I guess I do like her. Goodnight." Ann waves as Tom's car goes down the hill.[47]

That screenplay treatment for *First Father* is an outline for a full-length feature film. We'll venture some comments on it, then we'll identify the author and describe what happened to his treatment when it was circulated around the film industry.

First we'll try to provide something that is missing in the treatment itself as it stands—a one sentence summary of the theme. We'll begin with a simple synopsis of the story line:

A young doctor, recently returned from the Vietnam War, feels curiously restless and out of place in his placid Connecticut setting, and gradually a series of chance happenings set him on a search through his past until he makes an astonishing discovery about something that took place before he went off to that war.

So, the basic action of this plot line is a discovery action —which is one of the most powerful actions in all drama, someone trying to find something out. A discovery action underlies the greatest of all Greek tragedies, the *Oedipus Rex* of Sophocles. And like Oedipus, Tom begins in a curiously restless ignorance of the way things really are, until a peculiar set of circumstances force him to begin on a step by step search for the truth of what actually happened in the past.

There is always a good deal of Sherlock Holmes in any discovery action—the sniffing out of false leads, the picking up on insignificant clues, and the following through of one's hunches until one can figure out "whodunit." A deeper theme of this story line, then, is the truth versus conceal-ment, and how once one begins to question appearances and seek out an underlying reality, others will also become unwittingly caught up in that search as well. It's fascinating the way Tom's search triggers a similar search action in Sally, and unconsciously and indirectly, in Ann herself.

But because this discovery action is basically taking place inside Tom, the central theme of the story line will be an inner, and not an outer discovery—and the climax of the story will take place when both the inner and the outer discovery actions coincide, as they do in the scene at the Agricultural Fair. And because the real action of this story is inside Tom himself, it would take extraordinarily strong acting in the role of Tom to bring this film off successfully. Which is another way of saying, it would make a terrific star vehicle for some actor who really wanted to play the part of Tom.

The more we look at this treatment, the more fascinating it becomes. We could make a few comments on it that might heighten its potential as a major motion picture:

1. We might develop Tom's experience in the Vietnam War more specifically, to see why he is so peculiarly predis-posed to searching out some truth that is hiding behind appearances.

2. We might develop those first subtle glimpses of Ann, and see what unsettling images and fantasies and dreams they trigger for Tom.

3. We might develop such clues as Robertson's "honors history class," to reinforce the importance of the past in understanding the present.

4. We might develop that climactic moment where the real mother and father and daughter are brought together for the first time at the dinner party of the adoptive parents —instead of saying "The dinner goes off well," we might try to get as much mileage as we can out of this remarkably dramatic gathering, as it will surely be one of the high points of the film.

5. We might try to find some way to keep Tom and Sally from seeming to be so manipulative of Ann's adoptive parents, doing everything behind their backs. Granted it's a necessary part of the story line, but there does seem to be an element of contrivance in it.

6. We might want to tighten all the various complications and denouements of the story line, by staying closer to the basic theme of the treatment.

All of these comments are, in a way, an indirect compliment to the fascination of the screenplay treatment. Since it opens up so much in the way of character and story development, one wants to tinker with it endlessly to bring out all its potentialities.

Now we'll identify the author, and describe what happened to his screenplay treatment of *First Father*.

The treatment was written by Venable Herndon, who is a known screenwriter—he wrote the 1969 film *Alice's Restaurant* with Arthur Penn, a part of which will appear in the following chapter as a format model for a successful screenplay. His other credits include screenplays of *Too Far to Walk* for Otto Preminger in 1967; *Location* for Paramount, 1970; *Uncle Sam's Wild West Show* for United Artists, 1971; and

Jimmy Shine for Columbia, 1972. Venable Herndon has been teaching the screenwriting courses in the film department of New York University for many years.

Now for a description of what happened to his treatment of *First Father*. It would be nice to report that this treatment was picked up and was well on its way to being made into a major motion picture, but the truth is that Herndon's agent sent it around to studios and producers and independent filmmakers to see if anyone might be interested in commissioning a full-length feature film screenplay based on this treatment. And there were a few nibbles, and a couple of expressions of real interest here and there. Two or three readers sensed that a powerful screenplay could be developed out of this treatment, but for some reason they backed away from an outright offer. And curiously, there was a lot of negative feedback on the treatment, because something about the story seemed to scare people away. Comments ranged from "interesting" to "needs more development." One producer came close to putting his finger on the response problem, when he said that he "wasn't into adoption stories."

Not into adoption stories? But who said this was an "adoption story"? Clearly it is Tom's story, not Ann's, and as we said in our one sentence summary statement of the theme, it is a complex adventure in self-discovery, sort of a Connecticut Oedipus, and on an unconscious level this may be what was scaring so many people away from the treatment. The story line may have been probing too close to the primal psychosexual mysteries and secrets. After all, it's a curious unconscious coincidence that Tom is treating Ann for a broken ankle—the way Oedipus himself had had his ankles broken before he was given away to live with his adoptive parents. But then just because something is too close for comfort, it is no reason to give up on the thought of producing it. Nevertheless, when the *Oedipus Rex* of Sophocles was first produced in 425 BC, the Athenians did not vote it a first prize—because there must have been something about this greatest of all plays that was too close for comfort

111

as far as the Athenians were concerned. But for that very reason, we should think twice before rejecting out of hand any stories that might make us feel vaguely uncomfortable —that may be all the more reason for doing them, and giving them the first-rate production that they deserve.

Of course, we have no way of knowing whether this screenplay treatment of *First Father* would have fared any better, if Herndon had put in a summary statement of the theme at the beginning, to focus and guide a reader through the unfolding story line. Who knows, that might simply have intensified the unconscious resistance to the subject matter on the part of most readers. But at least then one would have the satisfaction of knowing, definitely, that the treatment was being rejected for its subject matter and theme, and not for any lack of story development. So as a general rule, we will still insist that one can't go wrong in putting a one sentence summary statement of the theme at the beginning of each screenplay treatment.

So, whatever became of this treatment of *First Father*?

Herndon told us that after about five years of trying to have his treatment picked up, he set it aside in his files and went on to other projects. Herndon has about 20 or 30 such treatments on file, proposals that have gone the rounds and have never been picked up for one reason or another. As we said, this is all a part of the screenwriting game and one can never afford to get discouraged about it.

For our purposes here, then, the screenplay treatment format is what really matters—and *First Father* gives us a good model for how a film treatment should be prepared: it presents a synopsis of the principal events of a story line, an indication of the outstanding visuals, a rundown of the characters, and a description of the crucial moments of the script. And for God's sake, don't forget to put in that one sentence summary statement of the theme at the very beginning!

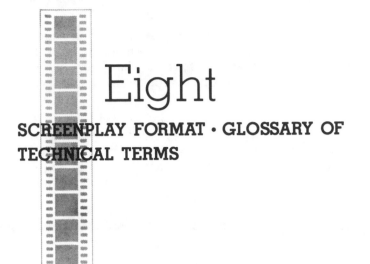

Eight

SCREENPLAY FORMAT · GLOSSARY OF TECHNICAL TERMS

What we said about screenplay treatments will carry over to the format of screenplays also—a good deal of the screenwriter's craft has to do with interesting agents and producers in his work, and so he should try to make the finished format as easy to read and exciting as possible.

Nothing is worse than a dull screenplay, and one cannot ever depend on a director or an actor or a producer to fill in for the screenwriter and provide the visual imagination to flesh out the various individual scenes of a film. It is part of the writer's challenge to make the work immediately effective, interesting, and powerful.

The goal is to write a screenplay that almost films itself as it is being read.

As one veteran screenwriter puts it:

It has to be read to get it made, so I've put a certain amount of brief description in it for the studio executives who are the first people to read it . . . to say, Ah, it takes place in an office, or in a park, or in an airplane. But I don't put in all kinds of directions in the writing that maybe other writers have to do. I just write dialogue with the briefest notation of where it takes place . . .[48]

Of course it is essential to master all the elements of the screenplay format. But on the other hand, one can go too far in this direction, and spend so much time on getting the format right that there's nothing left over but a lot of rote and lifeless writing. William Goldman voices a warning against doing things too much according to the letter of the law, in this complaint:

. . . The "proper" screenplay form, quote, unquote "proper," is that awful, stupid, moronic form where it says, capital EX . . . number . . . show numbers and then capital EXT for EXTERIOR BILL'S OFFICE . . . all that stuff. And why those peculiar things got into screenplays, I don't know, because that's really for when a movie's shooting . . .[49]

In other words, one can carry the whole thing too far, one can get so caught up in the "professionalism" of writing a screenplay, that one formats oneself out of all excitement and vitality.

Another hazard of overwriting a screenplay format is to insert too much directorial input—camera angles, interpretation, and instructions on the lighting and the set design. This reliance on too much technical information is a common mistake with beginning screenwriters. One must remember that the screenwriter's job is to tell the story, and if he tries to overload his screenplay script with a lot of technical paraphernalia, he will be spilling over into the fields of other professionals. It's always best to leave all of the technical decisions to the director, the production designer, the lighting man and the cameraman. The writer's job is to get the story told, as well as he possibly can. To underscore this point, it is sobering to read the following words by one of our greatest playwrights and screenwriters, Tennessee Williams:

In the writing of the film-script, I have rarely presumed to indicate to the director the camera-angles and the distance of the camera shots.[50]

So far as directorial indications and camera positions and scenic locations are concerned, we can leave it at this: if a particular technical effect seems especially important to the telling of your story, you can always try to write it right into the dialogue or the description of the events. For example, if you intend to create a sense of distance, you don't have to say "LONG SHOT"—you can always write, "In the distance we see two people getting out of a car" and leave it to the production people to translate this into technical terms.

At the end of this chapter, then, there is a glossary of technical terms for the screenwriter to use, if he feels that he must incorporate such things as camera angles and directorial input into his screenplay format. There are times when such technical indications are essential. But as a general rule the screenwriter should use such technical terms sparingly, and leave it to the production people to insert them later on. And they will, because once the screenwriter has finished writing his screenplay, then the production people will prepare a technical scenario which will be the director's own shooting script, and this shooting script will include all the necessary lighting indications, camera angles, visuals, sound effects, etc.

The screenplay, then, will simply present the essential story line, and it will be set down on the page in a special screenplay format according to certain basic guidelines. Incidentally, these basic format guidelines will be the same for a teleplay as they are for a cinematic screenplay.

The basic screenplay format guidelines can be summarized as follows:

115

1. Whatever camera indications and stage directions are required, should be typed across the page, margin to margin.

2. All dialogue should be typed within a 3″ wide column running down the center of the page.

3. The name of the character speaking should be typed just above the separate dialogue sections.

4. Any stage directions on how each character is speaking should be typed beneath the character's name and slightly to the left.

5. All dialogue and stage directions should be single spaced.

6. There should be a double space between speeches, and between all stage directions.

These basic screenplay format guidelines will be clear when one looks at the same screenplay pages which appear towards the end of this chapter.

These format guidelines are important, and they go a long way towards making a screenplay presentable to an agent or a producer. As one studio executive puts it:

Give it your best shot—when you submit something, have it in the form that is acceptable. Be as professional as you can—neat, clean copy. This is given a good saleable story—and once you've got that, present it in the most professional way you can. And: get a good agent.[51]

A word about length—screenplays should be 120 pages long, no more, and rarely less. That is the standard rule in the film industry, and some agents and producers say they will simply not look at anything that is longer or shorter than 120 pages. What is so sacred about 120 pages? It's because the script length of 120 pages equals a two hour full-length feature film—and that means the running time of each screenplay page is approximately equal to one minute of actual film time.

This is very different from dramatic playwriting, which averages out to about one minute per page for cold reading, but will open up to about two minutes per page for a full performance on stage. And this time difference between stage and film scripting tells us a good deal about the crucial difference between playwriting and screenwriting; it shows the radically different tempo and size and delivery of theatrical acting versus motion picture acting. As we said in an earlier chapter, events that happen onstage tend to be larger and require greater projection and more time than events that happen on film, which is of lesser magnitude and more immediate in terms of the pace of acting.

Screenwriting, then, averages out to about one minute per page, including all of the dialogue and stage directions and double spacing in between, if they are set down according to our basic format guidelines. And it's important for a screenwriter to observe this 120 page limit, as an entire film industry is geared to this standard screenplay formula.

Following are some sample format pages of the actual shooting script of a screenplay, and these pages can be used as a model for how the screenwriter should position his material on the page.

These are excerpts from the film script of *Alice's Restaurant*[52] by Venable Herndon and Arthur Penn, which is based on the song by Arlo Guthrie. We will reprint the title page of the screenplay, showing the correct format for the film title and the author and the date of creation and the copyright notice. Then we will print the opening two pages of the screenplay which set the tone and mood of the entire film and introduce the title and credits. Then we will print page 61 of the screenplay, to show what the format looks like in the middle of the film, during an especially interesting sequence of shots with voice over on the sound track. Finally we will print the last page of the screenplay, to show the format of the film's ending with indication of the closing title and credits.

Since these pages are from the actual shooting script which a director was using to make the film itself, there are a good many more indications of camera angles and technical effects than would ordinarily be found in most screenplay formats. We'll leave it to the reader to decide which indications he thinks are absolutely essential to the screenplay format itself, for the telling of the actual film story, scene by scene. As it stands, these pages are excellent examples of screenplay format, since they show the placement on the page of almost all the various notations that would ever come up in film scripting.

"ALICE'S RESTAURANT"

by
VENABLE HERNDON
and
ARTHUR PENN

1. INT: DRAFT REGISTRATION CENTER—DAY

A long line of eighteen year old boys moves worm-
like towards a steel desk commanded by a frumpy,
bespectacled lady clerk of fifty. As each boy
steps up he hands in a questionnaire which the
lady clerk checks meticulously.

>   LADY CLERK
>   (looking over glasses)
>   Johnson, Harold J.?

>   BOY
>   Oh—huh.

>   LADY CLERK
>   (fatigued, annoyed)
>   Didn't answer: "Do you know of any
>   reason why you might not qualify
>   for military service?"

>   BOY
>   Uh—uh.

>   LADY CLERK
>   (writing)
>   Okay. None. Next!

>   Next boy steps up.

>   LADY CLERK
>   Thee o—o—too—cop—oo—lous, George.

>   BOY
>   Uh—huh.

>   LADY CLERK
>   Didn't answer: "Other obvious phys-
>   ical characteristics that will aid
>   in identification?"

                              BOY
          Uh—uh.

     Lady clerk points to red and blue American flag
                 tattooed on left forearm.

                         LADY CLERK
          What's that?

                              BOY
          Oh yeah.

                         LADY CLERK
          American flag, left forearm.

                         (snapping)

          Next!

     MUSIC: Arlo song comes up underneath blurring
     Lady clerk's words, and we go into:

                         T I T L E S

     As titles end, Arlo steps up to desk. Lady
     clerk's automatic glance lengthens into an "I re-
     ally don't believe this one!" stare. Even in this
     lineup of boys (of every size, shape, color).
     Arlo, in his long ringlets and tall hat, stands
     out.

                         LADY CLERK
          Hat off!

               Arlo takes off his hat.

                         LADY CLERK
          Okay. What is this Huntington's
          Cho—ree—ah?

                    ARLO
          (makes himself tremble)
     The sha-a-a-kes.
               (stops trembling)
     Incurable nerve disease.

                 LADY CLERK
     And you have it?

                    ARLO
     Runs in my family. My father has
     it! My grandmother had it!

                 LADY CLERK
     It says here: "Do you know of any
     reason why you might not qualify
     for military service?'' Not your fa-
     ther! Not your grandmother!

                    ARLO
     I could get it.

- -
          76. INT: CHURCH-DAY

Everybody is singing and playing "Amazing Grace."
It has become a rocking, roaring revival hymn.

          Series of shots around church.

1) 2 or 3 people singing at the table which has a
    plundered, ravished look.

2) Girl passing joint to Jake who interrupts singing
    to take a deep drag.

3) Girl and boy feeding the burro a stalk of celery as
    they sing with all their might.

4) Ray and Alice climbing the stairs from the kitchen
    to their bell tower bedroom with Shelly watching
    Alice's legs disappear through the hatch. Hold on

122

Shelly's face as we hear the words: "Amazing
Grace, how sweet the sound, that saved a wretch
like me!"

77. INT: CHURCH—DAY—ANOTHER ANGLE

We look down from ceiling onto nave and apse to
see whole group singing, and then come down slowly on Arlo at the electric piano as he finishes
hymn with a resounding Amen, which fades into:

SOUND: strum of "Alice's Restaurant."

Arlo moves from electric piano on the altar plat-
form down into the nave, and takes Bob aside,
pointing as he does so to the rubbish heap in the
corner.

77A. ARLO AND BOB'S POV—RUBBISH HEAP

ARLO (V.O.)
(singing)
. . . and found all the garbage in
there and we decided that it'd be a
friendly gesture for us to . . .

78. EXT: CHURCH—DAY

Bob backs microbus up to the front door.
— —
196. EXT: CHURCH WITH ALICE IN DOORWAY—WIDE
SHOT

RAY (V.O.)
. . . wish we had 'em back . . . if
we'd just had a real place we'd a
all still been together . . .

CAMERA begins to move in on Alice.

123

                    RAY (V.O.)
        . . . without buggin' each other . . .
        we'd all be some kind of family . . .

Microbus motor fades away as CAMERA moves in
tight on Alice's face in its wilting crown of
flowers.

            197. FULL SCREEN—ALICE'S FACE

                    ARLO (V.O.)
                    (singing)
        You can get anything you want
        at Alice's Restaurant.
        You can get anything you want
        at Alice's Restaurant.
        Walk right in, it's around the back
        Just half a mile from the railroad
        track:
        You can get anything you want
        at Alice's Restaurant.
        Exceptin' Alice.

        198. INT: ARLO ON STAGE DURING CONCERT—NIGHT

                        ARLO
        'Stead of singin' "Alice's Restau-
        rant" let's sing Alice's favorite
        song.

Arlo starts "Amazing Grace" and lines it out
verse by verse to the audience which sings along
with him. Other performers come out from the
wings and join Arlo and the audience.

                T I T L E S

                FADE OUT

                THE END

124

As we said, these excerpts are from the actual final shooting script of *Alice's Restaurant*, and so they contain a good many more indications of the camera angles and the technical effects than would ordinarily be found in most screenplay formats. It's usually enough if the narrative stage directions indicate what is to take place, and leave it to the production people to designate that a particular camera shot should be "POV" (Point of View), or whether a certain sound effect should be "V.O." (Voice-Over). Those are usually directorial decisions and the screenwriter should be content to indicate the general effect that is desired.

However, the screenwriter should know the most frequently used technical terms in screenplay formatting, whether it is for his own final draft screenplay version, or the actual shooting script for the film.

Following is a glossary of technical terms in screenwriting, that may be used in setting up either a screenplay format or a final shooting script:

ANGLE	camera is on a person, place, or thing—either low angle shot, high angle "bird's eye" shot, or wide angle shot
CLOSE SHOT	camera is in on character—either full face, medium, or extreme
CRANE SHOT	moving shot by camera on mobile lift
CUT AWAY	shot that is used as insert, which deviates from the main action
CUT TO	transition from one scene to another
DISSOLVE	one image gradually replaces another onscreen
DOLLY SHOT	camera is moving, from a vehicle or is walked in—as opposed to

	pivotal pan shot where the camera is held stationary
ESTABLISHING SHOT	general view of area
EXTERIOR (EXT)	general view of area
FADE IN	image slowly appears dark to light
FADE OUT	image slowly disappears from light to dark
FLASHBACK	film cuts to some episode from a past story line
FRAME	a single strip of film
FREEZE FRAME	all action freezes, like a still shot
FX	technical sound effects, or visual effects
HOLD	action freezes
INTERCUT	back and forth between two or more shots
INTERIOR SHOT (INT)	room or corridor or hallway
JUMP SHOT	a shot is dropped from the ongoing action so the story line will seem to jump ahead
LONG SHOT (LS)	at distance—medium or extreme
MASTER SHOT	an overall view of the scene
MIRAGE SHOT	camera is deliberately out of focus
MOVING SHOT	camera is on the movement of the scene to follow an action
MONTAGE	a sequence of quick, related shots which are juxtaposed together to show some motif or theme
MUSICAL INTERLUDE	during a mime silent scene, music is heard on the sound track
OVER SHOULDER SHOT	camera is looking into the face of

	the other character, from the first character's vantage
PAN SHOT	camera moves from one location to another with a continuous movement, to create a horizontal or vertical panorama
POINT OF VIEW (POV)	a scene is seen from one character's perspective
PIVOTAL SHOT	camera is stationary, and makes a pan shot
PULL BACK TO REVEAL	camera moves away from image to reveal some new element
SCENE	shot or shots, one complete beat or action
SEGUE	bridge from one segment to another
SEQUENCE	series of related scenes
SERIES OF QUICK SHOTS	rapid cuts from one to another scene
SET-UP	camera or lighting position
SHOT	single piece of continuous film
SLOW MOTION	slow down film speed onscreen (which means speeding up film speed in camera), to create a dreamlike, slow motion, underwater mood or effect
SMASH CUT	a jarring sudden cut from one scene to another
SPEED UP MOTION	film speeds up rapidly onscreen (which means slowing down film speed in camera), to create rapid effect, opposite of slow motion
SPLIT SCREEN SHOT	picture divides into two or more parts

STOCK SHOT	some film is inserted from the archives, newsreel footage, etc.
STORY BOARD	planned shots on cards, drawings, laid out as in a comic strip
SUBLIM	a quick shot, perhaps a fraction of a second
SUPERIMPOSE	one image is overlaid on top of another
SWIRLING SHOT	camera moves around in a circle to take in the whole scene
TAKE	a shot or series of shots of a given scene of the story line
TIGHT SHOT	camera comes in on person or object
TILT UP TILT DOWN	camera is in the same position and pivots up or down
TRAVELING SHOT	camera moves to follow the events
TRUCKING SHOT	camera is on wheels and follows a moving object
VOICE OVER (V.O.)	narrator or character is speaking on sound track behind an image
WIDE ANGLE	camera includes a larger area of the scene
ZOOM IN ZOOM OUT	camera uses a zoom lens to make an image enlarge or diminish rapidly on the screen

After reading through the sample pages of *Alice's Restaurant*, and after looking over this glossary of technical terms, the next thing a screenwriter should do is keep on looking for more models to pattern his own screenplaywriting format after until he has mastered the formatting knack so thoroughly that he can confidently create his own unique style of creating screenplays on the page.

And along this line we should mention two titles, listed in the bibliography of this book, which are especially worthy of any screenwriter's attention. Both of these books contain outstanding screenplay format models that are useful and exciting for any screenwriter to consider.

The first book is William Goldman's masterful *Adventures in the Screen Trade*. Goldman is the author of such screenplays as *Harper*, 1966; *All the President's Men*, 1976; and *Marathon Man*, 1976. William Goldman insists that in all of his own screenwriting, he writes screenplays to be read by a reader, not by a film director or any other production person. And that may be Goldman's own way of avoiding the trap of cluttering up his screenplay format with a lot of elaborate and intricate camera instructions. He gives this blunt warning about not overloading the screenplay format with technical terms:

I talked to a star once who said, "You goddam screenwriters—putting in all that camera crap—trying to direct the picture is all you're doing. I *hate* all that camera crap. Just put down the words, I'll do all the rest."[53]

And Goldman has obviously taken this warning to heart, because all of his own screenplays are peculiarly free of "camera crap"—they read with a smooth and easy narrative flow that is as interesting for the reader to read on the page, as it is for a film audience to see it up there on the screen.

In *Adventures in the Screen Trade*, Goldman reprints the entire text of the screenplay version of his 1969 film, *Butch Cassidy and the Sundance Kid*, which starred Paul Newman and Robert Redford. And in reading through this screenplay format, it's interesting to witness how Goldman makes full use of the technical potential of film without cluttering up his screenplay with a lot of technical terms.

The film begins in a grainy black and white, with Butch Cassidy warily casing out a bank, then it cuts to a saloon where a game of blackjack is in progress and the Sundance Kid is suddenly accused of cheating at cards. After the conventionally tense eyeball to eyeball confrontation, the Sundance Kid shoots his opponent's gun belt off and keeps firing at it to make the belt whip like a helpless snake across the floor. Then the film follows Butch and Sundance out of town, and here is where William Goldman's screenwriting style shows itself in smooth and easy readable narrative flow, with no explicit camera indications:

BUTCH AND SUNDANCE riding. And as they ride, the FILM STARTS GOING INTO COLOR. Faint at first, then, as the ride goes on, stronger. By the end, the effect should be considerable, not only because we will be in full color at that time, but also because by then we will be at Hole-in-the-Wall.

CUT TO

CLOUDS. They are white, just like clouds ought to be, and they are fluffy enough and they hang there in the sky and then

PULL BACK TO REVEAL

BUTCH AND SUNDANCE riding along above the clouds, which spread out below them, filling a canyon. As BUTCH and SUNDANCE begin riding down into the clouds—

CUT TO

A SMALL HERD OF DEER, startled and scared, veering wildly off as BUTCH AND SUNDANCE come riding along.

CUT TO

BUTCH AND SUNDANCE continuing to ride. If before they were clearly somewhere high, they are now, just as clearly, somewhere low. They are working their way along a streambed that rises toward a distant crest.

CUT TO

BUTCH AND SUNDANCE riding along the crest, picking up their pace a little, because now they are getting there and

CUT TO

A ROCK FORMATION, strangely shaped, almost like a gated entrance to something, which it is: the entrance to Hole-in-the-Wall. And as WE DRAW NEAR,

CUT TO

HOLE-IN-THE-WALL. It is a sloping green valley, concave in shape, its upper rim coming in direct contact with a series of enormously high cliffs that rise almost vertically. At the bottom of the valley are a series of small lakes and streams.

CUT TO

BUTCH AND SUNDANCE, in the gated entrance made by the rock formation.

CUT TO

BUTCH. CLOSE UP, staring out at all the glorious desolation.

BUTCH
Ahhhhh: home.

And they start to ride down into the valley.[54]

There is tremendous economy and simplicity in this narrative sequence we have just quoted, and one must not be misled into thinking it is a simple thing to write so simply. Clearly the screenwriter had to visualize for himself the entire sequence of scenes before setting it down on the page, as if he himself were watching the finished film in his own mind. But once one has reached this level of screenwriting, one is clearly beyond the compulsion to set down the clutter

131

of technical terms and camera angles that will be trying to tell someone precisely how the film is to be shot. One can imagine that the above narrative sequence could be shot in any one of a dozen ways, all of them brilliant, all of them effective. What matters most of all is the ongoing narrative process of the writing, and that is the screenwriter's major concern.

The second book that is especially recommended for a screenwriter to compare format placement on the page is *Stopped Rocking and Other Screenplays*, by Tennessee Williams. These four screenplays by Williams are published posthumously, and they show this great playwright and screenwriter still endlessly exploring new styles and techniques of expression.

The book's editor, Richard Gilman, gives three examples from the recent screenwriting of Tennessee Williams —author's directions which are so poetic and impressionistic that it would be virtually impossible for any film director to translate them directly into specific cinematic terms. Here are the three directions:

1. This wide shot should have the appearance of a canvas by a master painter. I think of early Van Gogh and of the early Dutch schools—the emphasis on light and shadow. A poetic *tristesse*, on the surface, a stark desolation of the spirit under . . .

2. . . . trees that seem by their transcendent grace and lightness on a fair spring day to be undertaking to annihilate all sense and memory of the sprawling mass of the city.

3. This should not look like an ordinary bathroom . . . Color gives it a curious muted and melancholy radiance. Could it suggest a small apothecary shop near Verona at the time of Romeo's exile from that city?[55]

Granted that these three screenplay descriptions are more open and poetic and suggestive than they are explicit and technical and specific. But that is the whole point about the art of screenwriting when it comes to the idiosyncratic style of each individual screenwriter. It is the screenwriter's job to suggest in his own way what emotional and poetic effects should be taking place up there on the screen. And it will be up to others in the film industry to interpret the screenwriter's suggestions in specific cinematic terms of their own choosing. As we said about the William Goldman narrative sequence from *Butch Cassidy and the Sundance Kid*, one can also imagine each of these Tennessee Williams descriptions being shot in any one of a dozen ways, all of them brilliant, all of them effective.

This may seem to be a loss of creative freedom in one sense, but it is an enormous free achievement in another sense. Because, all one has to do is read through a number of excellent screenplays such as some of the work that has been excerpted here, and one will realize that the screenwriter has his own very special kind of freedom, which is the genius and power to visualize the final aesthetic effect that a film will have on a particular audience. We're not talking here about rewrites of individual lines, or changes in dialogue or characterization—those things are inevitable in filmmaking, but they now appear less of an insult to the screenwriter's art when they are compared to the larger overview of the film which is the screenwriter's proper provenance and vision of the work as a whole. That is his, and his alone.

And that's a pretty good rule to bear in mind, so far as screenplay formatting is concerned. Once the screenwriter has mastered all the basic format guidelines for layout and page placement of a screenplay, he should then feel free to develop his own style of open and ongoing narrative and descriptive writing flow that will suggest what the final film effect ought to be on the screen. And he should leave it to the director and the other production people to take it from there.

And that way, everyone will be happy.

Nine

MARKETING AND AGENTRY · CONTRACTS, UNIONS, COPYRIGHT PROTECTIONS, PLAGIARISM, PSEUDONYMS

In this chapter we will try to get down to some of the nuts and bolts of screenwriting and the marketing of screenplays.

We will describe the step-by-step process of how the screenwriter should go about preparing the physical copies of his screenplay; how he should go about claiming deductions for any expenses he may incur in the process; how he should go about securing copyright protection for his property, and how he can register it; how he should go about getting himself a good agent; what to expect from contract negotiations; where unions and writers' organizations can be useful to him; whether he should be concerned about the problem of plagiarism of his own work; and finally, when and why he might occasionally choose to use a pseudonym in association with his own work.

To begin with, a screenwriter has to have a physical property to offer. That is to say, after he is satisfied that he has written his screenplay as well as he is capable of writing it, and after he has set it down on the page according to the format guidelines, he will then need to have a master copy of the screenplay made. In addition, he will have to have duplicate copies of this master copy made so he can begin on the long process of promoting his screenplay.

If the screenwriter does not wish to type the final draft of the screenplay himself, he can find a competent typist to prepare a master copy of his 120 page script, according to the basic screenplay format guidelines. This may cost him around $100 for an excellent job of typing the entire screenplay. He should be sure to include with the master copy of his screenplay, a one page biography listing whatever credentials he feels are important to bring to the attention of whoever will be reading his script.

Then he will want to make duplicates of his master copy. Ten copies is probably the minimum number to make—one for his own personal use, two or three for copyright deposit and registration at a writer's union if he wishes, and then five or six to send on to any agent or producer he feels might be interested in the work. Actually it wouldn't hurt to make a lot more than ten copies, as the principal cost will be in preparing the master copy and then doing the initial duplicates—most copy places offer a reduced rate beyond the original five or ten copies made. And one never knows what opportunities might come up when an extra copy of the film script might be handy to pass on to an interested person. Certainly one should have enough copies to be able to circulate them freely among all the directors, producers and actors in the industry who might be helpful in getting them on to other persons who might be instrumental in making a sale.

So, the writer should take his master copy of the screenplay to a local xerox shop or offset press, and have the desired number of neat, clean, sharp copies made from it. We should say here that it's most important to have a high quality, professional job done on the xeroxing or offsetting, and not just some half-assed job, done in a slapdash way on some after-hours office machine by a well-meaning friend. A number of screenplay agents commented to us that any fuzzy, illegible xerox copy of a property will automatically prejudice any reader against the author's work.

Of course the cost and quality of good xerox or offset copying will vary from place to place and even from city to city, so it might be wise to do some comparison shopping first. But if the writer is planning to make more than 25 copies of his 120 page screenplay, he can probably count on spending another $100. And he may want to insert each xerox or offset copy in an attractive vinyl covering of some sort, to make each copy look as presentable as possible. And if we add on the cost for postage of mailing at either first class or book rate (depending on how fast the writer wants his copies to be delivered somewhere), we will be figuring on another $50 or so.

So the initial cost of typing the master copy ($100), plus the cost of xeroxing or offsetting about 25 copies ($100), plus vinyl bindings and postage ($50), will come to at least $250 per screenplay. And at today's prices that's a very modest estimate.

This may sound exorbitant for a screenplay property that hasn't even begun to make the rounds looking for a prospective buyer. It sounds terribly unfair? Unjust? Tell us about it. It's no more unfair or unjust than the investment of time and money that any other artist in any other field has to make: the painter has to buy his canvas and oils and pay his studio rent, the sculptor has to purchase his stone or marble and hire his models, the dancer and actor and musician all have to invest years of training in classes before they're ready to offer their skills on the open market.

Of course no one ever asked anyone to be a screenwriter, and there's still time to close this book and go out and get a good job selling insurance. But if the stakes don't scare you, and if our own sarcasm doesn't deter you, then you can always think of the extraordinary financial rewards if you're lucky enough to make a sale and your screenplay is made into a full-length feature film.

But money isn't really the issue here, is it? Because we know perfectly well that the painter and the sculptor, the dancer, the actor and the musician are all pursuing their separate arts with such heartfelt dedication and sacrifice of time and money, not primarily for monetary remuneration in the long run, but because these people really have no choice. They are artists because they are artists and they have a deep need inside themselves to perservere at their chosen craft. So why should screenwriters be any different?

Even so, money is always an issue that we can't ever reasonably ignore, so it's important to say this: the writer should keep receipts for every cent he spends on the furtherance of his screenwriting career. The best way to do this is to keep separate envelopes marked "XEROX" and "POSTAGE" and "STATIONERY" and "TYPING" and any other categories where he legitimately finds himself amassing bills, and when tax time comes each year, he should seek out a tax attorney who specializes in preparing income tax returns for artists and writers. A professional in the field will know all the appropriate deductions a writer is entitled to, and when a tax attorney has access to envelopes containing all the receipts for everything a writer has had to lay out cold cash for over any given year, he can claim the maximum deductions on the writer's behalf, and perhaps even claim a refund from the city, state, and federal tax agencies. A lot will depend on whether the writer is entitled to declare himself "self-employed" as a screenwriter, or whether his screenwriting is only a "part-time" activity—and that will be determined by how many sales of a writer's work take place in any given year, and what the total income from the writing amounts to. Any competent tax attorney can advise a writer in these matters, and it is certainly worth the fee he will charge for this service.

The next step in promoting the writer's screenplay, after he has had it typed and copied and retained receipts for tax purposes, will be to secure copyright. A writer can do this by writing to the Library of Congress in Washington and obtaining free forms to fill out and send in with one copy of his xeroxed or offset screenplay and a registration fee of $10.

The Copyright Revision Bill which Congress made operative on January 1, 1978, is a major comprehensive revision of the previous Copyright Law, and permits the United States to enter the Bern Union, which is an international organization which mandates copyright protection for the author's lifetime plus 50 years after his or her death. The most important thing to realize about this new United States Copyright Law is this: that copyright protection commences automatically upon the creation of a work. The actual designation of copyright notice on the manuscript, and the subsequent filing with the Library of Congress, are only formal registration procedures which are necessary to secure the protection of this law. But the copyright itself is automatic and begins when a writer actually creates the work, regardless of whether he ever files to secure that copyright protection or not.

The new Copyright Act of 1978 provides for the following different categories of work:

1. *Class TX*–Non-dramatic literary work. Includes fiction, non-fiction, poetry, periodicals, textbooks, reference works, directories, catalogues, advertising copy, and compilations of information.

2. *Class PA*–Works of the performing arts. Includes musical works, dramatic works, pantomimes and choreographic works, motion pictures and other audiovisual works.

3. *Class VA*–Works of the visual arts. Includes pictorial, graphic, or sculptural works, photographs, maps, globes, charts, technical drawings, diagrams, and models.

4. *Class SR*–Sound recordings. Includes records, cassettes, other sound recordings except for sound tracks of motion pictures and television, which are copyright under Class PA.

5. *Class RE*–Renewal registration. Includes all renewal reg-

istration for copyrights that are in the last calendar year of the first 28 year copyright term, and extends copyright protection for an additional 47 years.

Clearly, all or most screenplays will fall under Class PA, and a writer can obtain a free supply of PA forms by simply writing to:

> INFORMATION AND PUBLICATIONS SECTION
> Copyright Office
> Library of Congress
> Washington, D. C. 20559

The fee for an original registration of Class PA is $10, and the renewal registration is $6.00.

The copyright notice itself should be typed or printed on every copy of a work, in any of the following positions:

1. The title page

2. The page immediately following the title page

3. Either side of the front cover, or the front page.

The copyright notice itself should include the word "Copyright," the international symbol "©," and the year of creation or first publication, followed by the name of the author and/or owner of copyright. For example:

Copyright © 1985 by Eliot Morrison

This new 1978 Copyright Law mandates protection for a term of the author's life plus 50 years. In a work that is co-authored or jointly created, the copyright will continue for 50 years after the death of the last surviving co-author.

In addition to copyright protection, some writers may wish to prove not only that the work is theirs, but that they actually wrote it at a certain time. This is a more sophisticated form of protection and to secure this additional proof, they can register with the Writers Guild of America, which is the writer's union representing all writers who write free-lance television, film and radio scripts. The Writers Guild of America (WGA) has two branch offices, East and West, the dividing line being the Mississippi River. Following are the two addresses:

WRITERS GUILD OF AMERICA/WEST
8955 Beverly Boulevard
Los Angeles, California 90048

WRITERS GUILD OF AMERICA/EAST
555 West 57 Street
New York, New York 10019

Both branches of WGA offer a registration service, and if a writer sends $15, as well as a finished manuscript copy to either the East or West Coast branches, the manuscript will be deposited in the WGA archives, and no one will ever be able to take the manuscript out except the person who put it in there. In the event that a writer thinks that someone else may have stolen some of his own material—dialogue or story line or any other part of a screenplay—he can withdraw his manuscript from the archives and prove that on a certain date, his own written material existed in a certain form. As we said, this is a more sophisticated form of protection and is only important if a screenwriter feels he may want to establish the time and exact form of authorship, for evidentiary purposes in litigation. In all likelihood the beginning screenwriter does not have to worry about this sort of protection, at least not until he has developed and sold enough properties to make his work worth stealing on the open market.

The next step for the writer in promoting his screenplay, after he has made copies and secured copyright, is to try and obtain the services of a good agent. This is easier said than done, and of course it's all very well for guidebooks like this

141

to set down rules for what you should do and how you should go about doing it, as if the whole thing were some sort of recipe where all you have to do is follow the instructions to get the right results. We're well aware it's a pretty hellish and chancy world out there, and we don't mean to underestimate the element of risk, hard work and persistence that lie behind any completed project. All we can do is offer the best advice possible and then wish the writer Godspeed.

There are many listings of screenplay agents in the field, and the best thing a writer can do is obtain one of these lists and send out a sample mailing of individual letters to about 10 or 25 agents that the writer thinks might be right for his work. One such listing of screenplay agents is *The Screenwriters Guide: The Handbook for Film and Television Sales,* edited by Keith Burr and Joseph Gillis, with names and addresses of over 2100 producers and agents in this country and overseas. *The Screenwriters Guide* is published by Zoetrope Press, New York, and includes sections on how to see one's work, and how to make the best presentation of a property. The listing of screenplay agents indicates which agents are known to accept unsolicited manuscripts, which agents will only accept unsolicited manuscripts with references, and which agents are known to package film productions as well as represent individual clients.

One can also obtain listings of screenplay agents from the various writers' organizations, including WGA, and the Dramatists Guild of the Authors League in New York. And then, there is always word of mouth—a writer can always try to find out what agent represents other writers he may know and respect.

So it will be up to the individual screenwriter to compile his own personal listing of agents he thinks might be right for his work, and then prepare a mailing of inquiry letters to ten or twenty-five agents. This will mean a lot of letter writing, and a lot of wasted postage, and a lot of turndowns from a lot of unknown people. But the important thing is not to let oneself get discouraged, because this is the same kind of a challenge that actors have to face every day of the week when they go out on the rounds and do auditions for unknown casting agents and directors. They run into rejections nine times out of ten, or ten times out of ten if it's a bad week, yet they invariably find the stamina to go out and give it another shot the following week.

As one screenwriter commented to us: "You have to try everything that's possible—try every actor, every director, every agent, every contact—it's chaotic, it's haphazard."

What kind of letter should one write to the agents? Instead of coming up with our own guidelines, we'd rather let one of the leading screenplay agents answer this question. Bret Adams runs one of the most respected and successful agencies in the field, and he told us:

> We get so many unsolicited inquiries, that it becomes really an impossibility to even answer all of them. We do not answer any of them that do not at least have the self-addressed stamped envelope. And I'm talking about the letter now, it does help to have a recommendation from some source, someone that we've known in the past, whose recommendation might mean something to us. It could be the fact that we've worked somewhere. Initially, we would like to have a simple statement about what the property covers, what it is about, one page—it shouldn't be any longer, really.[56]

Let's take a very careful look at what Bret Adams is saying here:

1. The initial letter of inquiry must include a stamped self-addressed envelope.

2. The initial letter of inquiry should include a reference to someone who is related in some way to the agent.

3. The letter should include a one page summary statement about what the screenplay or the treatment is all about. No more than one page. Chapter Seven of this book

deals with how to write one-sentence summary statements of the theme or motif of a work.

We asked another agent the same question—what should a writer enclose in his initial inquiry approach to an agent, and Elizabeth Knappman of New England Publishing Associates told us essentially the same thing: enclose self-addressed stamped envelope, make reference to some person the agent would recognize, and include a summary statement of the work you are offering.

Suppose that out of your initial mailing to 10 or 25 agents, one agent responds to your proposed work and asks to see a copy of the complete text of the screenplay. And suppose further that the agent reads the screenplay and likes it, and offers to represent you. How can you know for sure that this is the right agent for you? Well, there's about as much guarantee as there is that the date you're planning for next Saturday night is right for you—there is no guarantee. But chances are if an agent responds positively to what you are writing and offers to represent you, it is some sign that there is the beginning of a sympathy and understanding that might develop in the course of a professional relationship. Of course it happens, rarely, that writers decide to switch agents, and that is always an option that one has.

However, even the best agency representation in the world will not guarantee that your work will move on to the next step and get sold. One has to be realistic about the nature of the market out there—it is erratic, unpredictable, and so fiercely competitive that sometimes bad things get accepted for the wrong reasons, and good things get rejected for no reason at all. And to make matters worse and even more bewildering, sometimes something that gets rejected by one person at one time, may very well be accepted by that same person at another time.

Sometimes the subject matter alone can work for or against a property, as we saw in Chapter Seven when a screenplay treatment was probably rejected for its underlying theme, and one producer commented that he was "not into adoption stories." This kind of thing can happen no matter how well developed a story may be. Bret Adams comments on this:

> We would respond at different times to different subject matter. I mean, if someone were to send us a script at this point about the plight of the poor farmer, we'd probably not be very interested because we happen to have a script like that that we're trying to sell, and there have been two or three that have been made . . .[57]

And Rosanne Ehrlich of Paramount Pictures agrees that subject matter can work for or against a particular property:

> There are definitely cyclical periods where certain subjects are of more interest—there is at the moment a real surge in teenage comedy, and we may move on to another part in the cycle where we'll be doing a lot of big historical adventures. It's definitely cyclical, there are different kinds of film that are called for at different times.[58]

Suppose now that a writer has been able to locate an agent who is interested in representing his work, and suppose this agent gets very close to making a sale of the writer's property to some studio or producer or independent filmmaker —what should the writer know about his role in closing any "deal"?

First, the writer should know that no responsible agent would ever dream of closing a deal without first checking back with the writer and getting his approval of the terms. The agent may say to the producer or studio or filmmaker, "It sounds fine to us, but let us get back to you after we talk it over with our client."

Second, the writer should know that the specific terms of any deal will depend a great deal on the nature of his property and the immediate needs of the marketplace at any given time. This accounts for the variability of terms in

145

different deals that are made in the film industry. There are probably a lot of other varying factors as well—the agent's ability to negotiate, the prestige of the screenwriter, how marketable a producer, filmmaker or studio feels the finished film will be, what the total budget is, etc. Nevertheless, we can still set down some minimum figures to show what kind of payments can be expected for a beginning screenwriter. As a general rule the minimum payment for a good screenplay treatment will range from $250 to $500 —although these are rough figures and could be much more. As for screenplays themselves, The Writers Guild of America publishes a schedule of minimum payments, as follows:

PAYMENT FOR SCREENPLAY, INCLUDING TREATMENT

	Low	High
1981	$15,873	$29,485
1982	$17,778	$33,023
1983	$19,734	$36,656
1984	$21,510	$40,000

Once a screenplay property has been sold to a producer, studio or filmmaker, there will be many other business aspects a writer will need guidance on, and here he can join one of the writer's unions such as The Writers Guild of America. In addition to getting the registration service we have already described in this chapter, the writer will receive full union benefits as WGA—a credit union, a hospitalization plan, major medical, informational services, a writers guild directory, a pension plan, and other associated services. At present the membership in WGA is about 3000; there is an initiation fee of $200, and annual membership dues of $50 a year, plus one and a half percent of gross money earned in the chosen area of free-lance writing. Some of the other writers unions and service organizations include The National Academy of Television Arts and Sciences, which gives the annual Emmy Awards, and The American Federation of Television and Radio Artists [AFTRA], which creates model contracts for the industry. There is also The Authors League, with its subsidiary organization, The Dramatists Guild. All of these organizations, incidentally, are excellent ways for the writer to stay in touch with his colleagues in the industry.

Once a screenwriter's script has been sold and goes into film production, the writer may wonder about the dangers of plagiarism. With so many different people having access to his material, and in such a highly competitive field as film production, the writer may be quite right to be concerned. However, if he has taken the proper steps to procure copyright protection, he has probably done all that he can do, legally, to safeguard against an outright infringement of his rights. We have already pointed out that the writer can take the added step of registering his original manuscript copy in the archives of WGA, but we doubted that this step was really in order for the beginning screenwriter.

In the following chapter we will describe the collaborative aspect of film production, and how the screenwriter must almost always expect to see his work changed, cut, tossed around, rewritten, and generally altered beyond all recognition—and there's nothing much the screenwriter can do about that because it just goes with the territory. But plagiarism is another matter altogether, and of course the writer has every right to try and protect himself against outright theft of his material. He should know, however, that from a legal point of view it's an extremely difficult thing to prove in court, beyond the mere "borrowing" or "influence" of one work on another work. To establish plagiarism or theft of material in a court of law, the writer would have to prove that not only was there a substantial part of any given work that had been quite literally copied, but the writer would also have to prove that there was criminal intention. And all this would have to be tried in court before a jury, to determine whether or not a criminal act of plagiarism had taken place. And as we say, this is an extremely difficult thing to prove.

But from an objective point of view, the overt instances of

plagiarism are rare. Agents and producers have told us that over the years that they have been working in the field of film work, they have never personally encountered any examples of plagiarism per se, although of course they all said they had heard stories about it taking place. Litigation for plagiarism is also rare, and is usually only of such clear-cut cases that there is a reasonable chance for there to be a favorable judicial decision.

This brings us to the last legal technicality of the screenwriting profession, and that is the use of pseudonyms by screenwriters. It's an odd fact that when one sees a movie, and sits through all those endless credits at the beginning of the film, when the writing credit appears on the screen, it may not be the real name of the screenwriter at all, but a false name, chosen by the author because he does not wish his real name to appear for any one of a number of reasons.

One reason for a screenwriter's use of a pseudonym is purely historical and involves one of the ugliest periods of political interference that ever occurred in the film industry. When the House Un-American Activities Committee held hearings in the late 1940s to determine which people were working in the film industry who might have Communist sympathies or be members of what HUAC deemed to be a Communist front organization, there was a shock wave that was felt throughout films for several decades afterwards. Because, at those HUAC hearings, many names were named by so-called "friendly witnesses," and many substantial careers were wrecked by the merest tinge of guilt by association.

Otto Preminger tells the story of this disgraceful era in his autobiography, *Preminger:*

> It began in the spring of 1947 when the chairman of the House Un-American Activities Committee, J. Parnell Thomas, came to California to look for Communists. It was an old hunting ground for him. He believed the entertainment industry to be a breeding ground for sedition. He had once attacked the Federal

Theatre as a hotbed of "Communism and the New Deal."

He talked to people about the Screen Writers' Guild, which indeed had a number of members who attended Communist cell meetings. Membership in the Communist Party was legal, but most of those who attended the meetings or joined the Party were actually liberals who thought that some aspects of Communism would relieve social justice. They had no intention to overthrow the government.

Congressman Thomas returned to Washington with some names and his committee began to subpoena writers to testify if they were, or ever had been, members of the Communist Party. If they refused to answer they could be charged with contempt; if they answered in the negative some of them exposed themselves to charges of perjury; if they answered in the affirmative they were required to name others.

Ring Lardner, Jr., was one of the first to be summoned. Lardner was a gifted screenwriter who won an Academy Award in 1942 for the Katharine Hepburn-Spencer Tracy film *Woman of the Year*. He interrupted work with me on the script of *Forever Amber* to go to Washington. His testimony before the congressional committee is full of interruptions. He refused to discuss whether or not he had been a member of the Communist Party. As a descendant of one of the Minutemen at Lexington he didn't see how he could be labeled un-American. What he tried in vain to read into the record was a statement that the committee was behaving in an un-American way by attacking the freedom of American citizens.

Studio heads, alarmed at the possibilities of guilt by association, met secretly at the Waldorf-Astoria in New York and drew up a list of screenwriters, directors, producers, and performers that they believed to have Communist sympathies. It was agreed that everyone on the list would be fired and blacklisted.[59]

Ring Lardner, Jr., and nine others became known as the "Hollywood Ten," and they were all sent to prison. In time the industry blacklist grew to over 400 names, all of whom were secretly dropped from studio employment. Many reputable screenwriters found themselves unemployable: some became alcoholics, some committed suicide, some dropped out of the industry completely. But in time some screenwriters could continue working provided they waived onscreen credit for their work and allowed a pseudonym to appear as the writer of record.

Incidentally it was Otto Preminger who finally broke the Hollywood blacklist, in 1957, when he hired Dalton Trumbo to write the screenplay for *Exodus*, adapted from the novel by Leon Uris. Trumbo was another of the "Hollywood Ten" and since his release from prison he had been writing screenplays under a pseudonym and sometimes getting a pittance fee of $1000 for each finished film script. In fact, under the pseudonym of "Robert Rich," he actually won an Academy Award in 1957 for his screenplay of *The Brave Ones* and was not even able to go up onstage to receive his Oscar. Otto Preminger changed all that when he told United Artists in 1959 that he was going to put Dalton Trumbo's real name onscreen as the author of the *Exodus* screenplay, and there was nothing the studio could do about it. From that moment on, other screenwriters who had been blacklisted were able to stop using pseudonyms and get full credit for their work using their real names.

But there is another reason for the use of pseudonyms by screenwriters, and that reason will probably exist for as long as there is a film industry. One screenwriter, Eleanor Perry, describes a circumstance where she would not allow her real name to appear onscreen, and instead opted for the use of a pseudonym:

> I didn't want to show that as my work. It was the work of a bunch of business guys sitting in an office, and sometimes their wives or their girlfriends . . . that's the most astounding thing. You know, that . . . I'm constantly hearing, Well, you know, this brilliant girl I'm

shacked up with, she read your script and *she* doesn't think that could possibly happen. *She's* never heard of that happening. And you're sitting there, you know, the professional presumably, hearing what . . . and tomorrow he'll be shacked up with another girl and have another opinion . . .[60]

This is a perfectly legitimate protest on the part of a distinguished screenwriter, someone who has worked hard on a property and has seen it so altered that it bears little resemblance to what she originally conceived. So now she wishes to dissociate herself from the project, yet still receive remuneration for the work she has done on the film.

And in fact, The Writers Guild of America has a registration service for pseudonyms, to take care of just such a situation. WGA told us:

Often we get requests, and people register their pseudonyms here. They can use pseudonyms for various reasons—if they don't feel it's their material, or it wasn't what they wrote, or whatever, but still they want to get compensation for it.[61]

It is true that actors usually use pseudonyms, but for a different reason—they choose interesting names like Tony Curtis and Cary Grant and John Wayne, because the real names like Bernie Schwartz and Archie Leach and Marion Morrison wouldn't sound so good at the box office. But it's just a shame that some screenwriters have to choose pseudonyms because sometimes they're too ashamed to have their own real names up there on the screen, attached to a particular property.

We began this chapter by saying we would get down to the nuts and bolts of screenwriting—all the physical and economic and legal considerations that come up once a writer takes his screenplay into the open marketplace. There is one last practical matter we should point out.

If, as some agents and producers have pointed out in this

151

chapter, the market for certain screenplays is obviously cyclical, with certain subject matter more in demand during one year and certain other subject matter not at all in demand during the following year, then it's important for the screenwriter to recognize the unpredictability of the market in this regard. And that means if he is not able to sell one of his film scripts in any given year, he should keep trying with it on the following years. And he should also maintain a file system of all his past work, including film scripts he may have written many years ago, so he will be able to keep them in good condition and know where they are so he can pull them at a moment's notice to send out when he thinks they might find a more favorable market.

The film industry is, as we said, pretty erratic and cyclical and unpredictable—and that's all the more reason for the screenwriter to keep his own materials in excellent order, stored in clean, dustfree and carefully indexed file cabinets, so he will be able to stay one step ahead of the game at all times.

Ten

COLLABORATION · THE SCREENWRITER AND THE REST OF THE FILM INDUSTRY

The sobering reality of the film industry is that a screenwriter must not only know his own craft, but must also have some working knowledge of the various other crafts that go into the making of a motion picture. And that means he must know when and how he must cooperate with, and occasionally yield to, the producer, the director, the actor, the cameraman, the scenic designer, the lighting technician, the editor, the music director, and sometimes even the makeup artist and the script supervisor. Because all of these people are also important in the collaborative art of the filmmaking process, and only when all of these people are working together harmoniously on the common project of making a movie can there ever be anything like a true artistic consensus in the finished film.

Of course, the same kind of collaboration is also required in the theatre, and in opera, and in dance, and in many of the other performing arts—but there is probably no creative enterprise where an artist is more dependent on the skills of

153

his fellow artists than in screenwriting. There is an entire industry behind the shooting of any one film, and the screenwriter must always be aware of this vast community of interests that he is working with.

You can get some idea of the truly interlocking nature of film production if you think of some recent film you may have seen, and then try to separate out the various contributions that were made by the various craftsmen who were at work on this one film. Can you definitely say for sure where the screenwriter's work left off and where the actor's work took over? Or can you single out the input of the director, or the cameraman, or the film editor, from the input of the screenwriter? In other words, can you really be sure that you know who contributed what, after you've seen any given film?

Oh well, you may say, you're only a layman and you may not have all that much experience in filmmaking—but surely someone who has spent an entire lifetime in the field could tell whose contribution went into which scenes of a film? Well, we asked this question of Joan Fontaine, the distinguished actress who has worked with such other distinguished actors as Laurence Olivier and Judith Anderson in *Rebecca;* and with Norma Shearer and Rosalind Russell in *The Women;* and who received the Academy Award in 1941 for *Suspicion,* with Cary Grant and Dame May Whitty, directed by Alfred Hitchcock. We asked Miss Fontaine:

> When you see a film, can you tell the work of the screenwriter from the work of the director or the work of the actor?

And Miss Fontaine answered:

No.

And then we asked, if *you* can't tell, with all your wealth of background and experience, then how can the average filmgoing layman tell? And Miss Fontaine answered:

How can a *critic* tell?—that's the main thing, how can a critic ever sit down and say it was great direction or great writing or this line is superb or that actor when he did this—how can a critic say that, how can he know whether the director made the line up, or whether the producer came in and said to the director, why don't you move it all over on one side of the stage—so the critic thinks that's all a brilliant piece of directing![62]

In other words, you can never really tell who made what contribution in a finished film, and that's probably as it should be in such a great collaborative art form as film-making. You probably can only come up with a few instinctive rules of thumb. One screenwriter told us that he could usually spot certain things when they were working extraordinarily well or extraordinarily badly:

You can see direction when it's brilliant, and you can see dialogue when it's bad, and you can see acting when it's not working—but when it's all working together, it's mysterious . . .[63]

And it's that mysterious working together that is the collaborative genius of filmmaking, and the interlocking nature of all the various crafts that go into the making of a really good motion picture.

But this collaborative aspect of filmmaking is also what usually gives the screenwriter so many of his worst headaches. Why is he always the one who has to stand aside and watch his best work get changed or cut or rewritten or turned utterly upside down? Because it usually does happen that way—in fact, changing a screenwriter's own original work is most often the rule, and not the exception.

There are many reasons for this, and some of them have to do with the peculiar circumstances of film production. Here is a description of what can go on during the shooting of a film that will make changes in a screenwriter's work almost inevitable:

155

Sometimes, when an important actor can only be present for the first, middle, or last weeks of the shooting schedule, all of his or her scenes will be bunched together, regardless of location or light considerations. The resulting sequence solves budget problems, logistical problems, career problems, union problems, but it has nothing to do with reinforcing the flow of the story.[64]

Now if the flow of the story line is not in the hands of the screenwriter at all times, due to the peculiar nature of the filmmaking procedure, then a very subtle thing takes place —the subtext of the work begins to belong more to the director and the actor than it does to the screenwriter. Because when a production schedule becomes so discontinuous that it makes the shooting sequence topsy turvy, then it will be up to the director and the actor to hold onto the inner continuity of the story line. And once the subtext of the story line is taken out of the hands of the screenwriter, his role in originating the filmscript will be automatically diminished, and his authority as author of the story line will thereby be undermined, and he will begin to feel more and more like a subordinate figure, perhaps even a hack, a lackie, and a dispensable part of the filmmaking process.

But as we said at the outset, this is the sober reality of the film industry, and the screenwriter had better be aware of it from the start. As one major studio told us:

It's naive to expect that in a collaborative medium there will not be input from the studio, the producer, the stars, the director—that's what the medium is, it's a collaboration. And to believe that your work will be put on the screen as it was originally written, doesn't really show an understanding of the process.[65]

And behind the need to work collaboratively with all of one's fellow artists on a film project, there is another major consideration that will be operative on every motion picture. That is the budget, which will make itself felt on every level of filmmaking. There is probably no field of art where the execution of an author's work entails so much cost risk to so many other people as it does in films. As one agent told us:

There's a basic cost in making a film that doesn't change, whether or not it's a star vehicle or non-star. There is the cost of the camera, and the equipment, and the film itself, and the sound. In the theatre, you can do workshop productions somewhere for almost nothing, or you can do a reading for very little, or form a small company in Boston or Vermont. But the hard thing for a screenwriter is that there's no way to start small and grow up with the film business. There's no such thing as non-profit films.[66]

Hence the screenwriter's work will not only be subordinate to the artistic consensus of his fellow workers, it will also be severely affected by budgetary considerations. And under these enormous pressures, the craft of screenwriting becomes one of conciliation and compromise and endless rewriting and rewriting and rewriting. As Robert Towne comments:

The fact of the matter is that everything has to be rewritten in movies. Almost every day. Rewrites are inevitable.[67]

And even if a screenwriter accedes to this need for endless rewriting when a film goes into production, there may still be a subtle and psychological conflict that will build up in the form of an adversary relationship between the screenwriter and the director, to see who will retain control of the script. And of course in this kind of a conflict the director will always win, on every point that comes up, since filmmaking is, in fact, the director's medium.

157

But if we said that filmmaking was such a great collaborative venture, how can we turn around now and say that it is a director's medium?

Of course it depends on the studio, or the producer, or the independent filmmaker as to how much overall power and control any one individual director may exercise over any given film script once it goes into production. At the one extreme there is the "auteur" theory of filmmaking, which says the director himself is the true "author" of a film. Excellent European filmmakers like Bergman, Truffaut, Fellini, and others would conceive of an entire film as a part of their total art, and they would not make any strict distinction between the separate functions of directing and writing and editing—it would all be part of a single overriding instinct which would be authoring the finished film.

In America, the directors who come closest to embodying this "auteur" approach to filmmaking would be people like Charlie Chaplin, Orson Welles, Woody Allen, and Alfred Hitchcock, who would all conceive each film down to its smallest detail. Hitchcock especially would work out every aspect of the film in his own mind before he even began work on the actual writing of the screenplay script—and then he would hire screenwriters to put his preconceived ideas into cinematic form. This was not as rote and mechanical as it sounds, nor did it produce lifeless and mechanical films—Hitchcock was a great artist and knew better than anyone else what he wanted to achieve and how he could best go about achieving it. And it was no idle whim on Hitchcock's part that he liked to personalize each of his films by making a cameo appearance himself in some insignificant role. It was like leaving his own fingerprint somewhere on the film, as evidence to show that he, and he alone, was the true author of the film.

There are less extreme approaches than the "auteur" directors, but they are approaches which still exercise an inordinate degree of control over the making of films. There are, for example, the producer-writers, who not only write the script but also oversee its eventual production—people like Nunnally Johnson, Joseph Mankiewicz, Robert Rossey, John Huston, and Billy Wilder. Then there are the producers who pride themselves on working directly with the screenwriter—people like Hal Wallis, whose work includes the early 1932 film *I Am a Fugitive from a Chain Gang,* and extends all the way through the 1953 film *Come Back, Little Sheba* and the 1961 film, *Summer and Smoke.* Wallis comments that if he ever buys an original story from a writer, he devotes a lot of time to conferences with that writer in order to develop the screen treatment so it will be exactly the way he, Wallis, feels it has to be when it goes in front of the camera. And then there are the film directors who work in the same way with the screenwriter—people like Otto Preminger, who spent several hours every day working with his screenwriters until a script was finished. Preminger comments that some film directors do this and get a writer's credit on the finished film, but Preminger himself has never claimed the credit because he feels it is all a part of his job as the film's director.

Of course under these circumstances a screenwriter will sometimes complain that others are exercising inordinate control over his own work. But he must realize that, once he has sold a screenplay, it is no longer "his own work" in any legal sense of the term. It's a little like selling a car to someone and then complaining that the new owner has painted it red. Because that sale constitutes a legal transfer of property rights, and the new owner has every right to do anything he wants with the car.

The screenwriter should also realize that it is not only the film directors, but also the film producers who will often have preconceived ideas of how a film should turn out, and they will not hesitate to inject their own notions into the screenwriting process. Joan Fontaine sums this up succinctly when she says, "Every producer thinks he's a writer," and she goes on to describe the power that major stars who were also acting as producers could have over others in the

159

industry, sometimes pitting one set of writers against another set of writers:

> I did the Bob Hope show, and I worked with Bing Crosby where his writers were on the set constantly, and would come up and whisper, and he'd say, "Hey that's a great idea—okay, we're going to do this now!" And the latest gag that occurs to his gag-writers is put right in on the spot, regardless of who the director or the producer is. The power of Hope and Crosby was so large that even Billy Wilder, who was no mean writer himself, was overruled. "It's either this way or goodbye boys, I'm going out to play golf until you've seen it my way"—And he did, too. And that's it, that's power.[68]

At this point, the screenwriter is probably wondering if there is any legal remedy for this state of affairs. The Writers Guild of America admits that it can do nothing to protect the interest of the writer in such a situation. WGA comments,

> If you're writing a program, with a variety of financing that's going into it, involving an enormous number of people, one of the unfortunate realities is that dealing with that much money—well, things tend to get rewritten, as angry as we are about it.[69]

And when the writer's union admits this, the doors are left wide open for even uglier instances of abuse against the screenwriter. One of the most poignant accounts of the writer as hack, as hired lackie who is a pawn in some colossal power struggle in films, is in the following brief description of life in the film industry:

> Trying to get ahead in Hollywood was like living in Rome under Caligula. That's what the power people were like. They would give you some disgusting, humiliating task to perform and then punish you as an

unworthy person for doing something so degrading. Of course, if you didn't follow orders, you were beheaded for disobedience.[70]

And there are those who will describe the screenwriter as the lowest of the low, the vermin among the ermine. One screenwriter told us that after all his years in Hollywood, if he were to do it all over again he would be a director because, he said, that was the only real artistic function that had any clout. "Being a writer," he sighed, "is like being someone's wife—it's hideous, in terms of power."

Certainly those screenwriters who have been able to survive within the industry must have a capacity for adapting to these terrible pressures of collaboration, and they must also have an innate genius for rewriting, usually on the spot. Rewriting has been called the one survivable art for the screenwriter, the one indispensable skill he must have at his disposal. Only a very young or a very inexperienced screenwriter will imagine that his final screenplay version will go on to be the final shooting filmscript. Age and experience teach the necessity to adapt and revise according to the changing needs of the situation.

This may evoke cynicism in some screenwriters, or then again, it may result in a wise resilience that is the chief virtue of a good screenwriter. Otto Preminger claims that Ben Hecht was an excellent screenwriter precisely because Hecht had such contempt for the profession. "He really felt that film work was beneath him," Preminger says, and one can sense the Olympian detachment that Hecht must have had towards a profession that he excelled at just because he did despise it so much.

Of course the extreme pressure of collaboration will take place only if the writer himself is on the film set. And this will vary from producer and director. If a screenwriter is young and inexperienced, the producer will not want to negotiate a per diem expense, plus transportation and all the rest, just to bring him on location so he can hang around and get upset as he watches his work being altered. And the director will not want him around if the screenwriter is not able to rewrite on the spot, which is the only real reason for having a writer on location. Generally speaking, it will only be the veteran screenwriters who will be allowed on location, because their value to the film company has already been demonstrated by their ability to make instant rewrites on demand.

Now we have said a great deal in this chapter about the negative aspect of collaboration in filmmaking, especially as it pertains to the role of the screenwriter. And we have said all these things because the writer should be well aware of the nature of the film industry he will be working for; he should have no illusions about the sanctity of his own work under such extraordinary circumstances.

And he may feel that the screenwriter is unduly persecuted by his own industry. Because after all, in the legitimate theatre the playwright is protected by the Dramatists Guild contract which specifies that no one can ever change a single word of an author's play script without first getting his consent. But there is no such contract that pertains to a screenwriter. Whether he is working for a studio or a producer or an independent filmmaker or for television, the screenwriter is considered an artist for hire, and that means his own work will always be subordinate to the needs of a larger reality.

But in fact this is not much different from what actually takes place in the theatre. Most theatrical productions put so much pressure on the playwright to cut and edit and revise, that—Dramatists Guild contract or no—the playwright will usually have to give in and compromise on most of the same issues that a screenwriter will have to. So in practice it usually works out to the same thing; the only difference is that in the theatre a playwright *may* have to compromise, whereas in films the screenwriter will *always* have to compromise.

So by this time the reader should not have any romantic fantasies about how some producer will come along and buy his screenplay and film it in exactly the same form that he has written it. Because, in reality, it simply never happens that way.

But with all of that said, we can now go on and say that there is also an extraordinarily positive side to a screenwriter's collaboration in the film industry. There would have to be, otherwise no screenwriter in his right mind would remain in the business, no matter what the financial rewards may be. And there are too many distinguished screenwriters who have been at work in the industry for decades, and who still love the work and feel stimulated by the circumstances of screenwriting. So this is the appropriate place to describe what that extraordinarily positive side of screenwriting is all about.

Sometimes when a group of exceptional artists are gathered together on a single film project, and sometimes when the fates are kind and the weather is right and the breaks are in the air, then sometimes an authentically miraculous thing may take place. And when this miraculous thing happens, it more than makes up for all of the heartache and hysteria that any individual artist may have suffered on any one of a number of demeaning film projects. In fact, this miraculous thing is enough to restore anyone's faith in filmmaking as one of the most exalted art forms ever conceived by the mind of man.

But rather than get overly rhapsodic about it, let's take a look at a very specific example of a film project where this miraculous thing was quite obviously happening to all of the individual artists who were at work on the making of a particular movie.

We'll take as our example the 1954 film of *On the Waterfront*, and, from interviews with some of the key people and one or two outside observers, we'll try to piece together some impression of what went on in the collaborative process of the making of that film—and show how "the miraculous thing" was happening for all of the individual artists at work on the film.

On the Waterfront was directed by Elia Kazan, screenplay scripted by Budd Schulberg, musical score composed by

163

Leonard Bernstein, and the film starred Marlon Brando, Eva Marie Saint, Rod Steiger, Lee J. Cobb, and Karl Malden. The film is an overwhelming exposé of life on the New Jersey docks, as it focuses in on the workers and their bosses and the crooks who try to muscle in on the waterfront action. The story line pits one man's integrity against the suffocating corruption that is all around him, and Marlon Brando's performance has to be one of the most searing portrayals ever captured on film—Brando is alternately subtle, brutal, poignant, harrowing, and lyrical in his heroism.

You could say a lot of things about the chemistry that went into this particular grouping of artists. Kazan is famous for his ability to elicit the finest work from his colleagues, imperceptibly touching them in ways that will unlock some hidden genius they may not even have known they were harboring. Brando was at the height of his early success in films, having made, a few years before, the definitive portrait of Stanley Kowalski in *A Streetcar Named Desire* opposite Vivian Leigh, a film which was also directed by Kazan. Some actors in the *Waterfront* company, like Rod Steiger and Eva Marie Saint, were being given their first major chance to show how strongly they could perform under the best of circumstances. Others in the company, like Karl Malden and Lee J. Cobb, were veteran actors who brought a wealth of technical experience to their roles. And of course all of these artists—director and actors alike—were bound together by a mutual sense of style, an extreme American social realism that was so specific it almost seemed to be improvisatory in its performance. This style is one of the great legacies of the American theatre tradition and has its roots back in the Group Theatre of the 1930s where the plays of Clifford Odets provided the foundation, consciously or unconsciously, for some of the great performances that happened in *On the Waterfront*.

Of course the acting performances are what stand out in *On the Waterfront*. Here is Billy Wilder talking about one of the most famous scenes from the film, when the two brothers are talking together in the back of a cab, and the

Brando character begins accusing his brother, the Steiger character, of having betrayed him when he was trying to be a prizefighter—and he reproaches his brother with the pathetic outcry, "I coulda been a contender." This scene is so deservedly famous, that few people have noticed something extraordinary about the camera work in the scene, which Billy Wilder points out:

> One of the best scenes I've ever seen in a picture was between Brando and Rod Steiger in *On the Waterfront*, where they are sitting in a cab—not even a transparency in back: they didn't have it, they wanted to save money; instead they had Venetian blinds on the window of the cab; nobody cared. The camera was there and the two brothers were talking, especially Brando, beautifully and very well written. It was a scene that lasted seven minutes, no cut, no close-ups, no nothing: one of the greatest scenes, because you were involved.[71]

What a remarkable thing!—the camera was stationary throughout the entire scene, and the scene carried powerfully because of the greatness of the acting, directing, and screenwriting.

And in fact this is one of the rare instances where a screenwriter can report that the scene was played exactly as he had originally written it in the screenplay, word for word, with no changes or cuts or alterations of any of the lines. We have Budd Schulberg's word for it:

> I remember with Marlon Brando in *On the Waterfront*, that he was kind of screwing up some of the lines. But he is awfully creative and often he can improve the lines. But, at the same time, he can also fuck up a favorite line. And sometimes he would do that, and sometimes he would make it better than what I had done. I still believe in a script, I will always believe in that. Despite all the talk about the "improvised taxi scene," that scene was played exactly as written. Kazan

165

THE ART OF SCREENWRITING

balances cinematic inventiveness with loyalty to the
script. At the same time, I do feel that improvisations
can co-exist, but the writer, unless he is involved in the
making of the improvisation, is being tampered with
too much.[72]

This also is remarkable!—anyone who has seen *On the
Waterfront* will marvel that that taxi scene was being played
word for word, exactly as the screenwriter wrote it, with no
improvisational changes or insertions made by either of the
actors. Yet here we have the screenwriter's own word for it. It
makes the scene seem even more brilliant, knowing that the
actors were abiding by the original screenplay film script.

That's not to say that the creative genius of a great director
like Kazan, or the irresistible talent of a great actor like
Brando, can't often open up a screenplay text and add a
dimension that might not have been there in the original
screenplay. Here is Budd Schulberg reporting that just such
an example of collaborative magic did take place elsewhere
in the filming of *On the Waterfront*, where the Brando
character is walking along with the Eva Marie Saint character. Schulberg reports that Kazan tried interpolating his own
stage directions, which completely opened up the intention
of the scene, and for the better:

I would try to indicate the general idea of the action, but
often it was done much better than I had ever conceived
it. I think one good example would be the love scene
between Marlon Brando and Eva Marie Saint in the park
in *On the Waterfront*. In the script, as I remember it, I had
them pretty much walking along together. The dialogue
went more or less back and forth, and it was pretty
good. But Kazan did a great many physical things with
that. He sort of separated them. He would have her step
on a swing or go far ahead or pick up a glove. He would
move them in and out from each other through the
park, so it wasn't just a shot of two people talking as
they moved through the park. When I watched it being

made I was impressed with these innovations that made the scene that much better. I do think that something was taken away from the verbal interplay, but the way the scene was staged and shot gave it a greater emotional impact.[73]

Of course it takes considerable maturity and not a little magnanimity on the part of any screenwriter, to admit that anything an actor or a director might add onto his own original screenplay script was, in fact, a decided improvement, instead of sulking over what a conscienceless infringement had been perpetrated on the work. But Schulberg is a veteran screenwriter whose work includes the scripting of the 1939 *Winter Carnival*, the 1957 *A Face in the Crowd*, and the 1958 film *Wind Across the Everglades*, and he is also an author who saw his tough 1956 novel about the fight game, *The Harder They Fall*, go through the process of adaptation into a screenplay by Philip Yordan to become a major motion picture with Humphrey Bogart, Jan Sterling and Rod Steiger. So Schulberg knows enough to yield when yielding is in order, and that is really what collaborative screenwriting is all about.

Before we close this chapter on collaboration in the film industry, we should give one last example of how one film craft can enable another film craft to rise to inspired heights through simple encouragement and suggestion. We'll use the same film, *On the Waterfront*, to show how the same miraculous thing, the same collaborative magic between director and screenwriter, even extended over to the director's influence on the cameraman. Here is James Wong Howe, talking about how he filmed the crucial last scene of the movie:

Then Kazan said, "Now I need a shot of Brando. He's been beaten up, so he's dizzy and he's walking into the warehouse as the door opens." We shot that with his feet staggering and a close-up of him: we had a handheld camera, an Eyemo, and I gave it to the operator. I

167

put a chalk mark on the cement and said, "Now look through that camera and walk around that chalk mark." He said, "Gee, I'm getting a little dizzy." I spun him around and said, "Keep walking. Keep walking." He said, "I'm dizzy." I said, "OK, now point the camera at that door, hit the trigger, and walk." It photographed, you see? He couldn't walk very steady, so it made a wonderful shot to reflect how Brando was staggering.[74]

Only in an authentically free atmosphere of risk and trust and creative adventure could a cameraman have dared to make such a bold experiment, and only with something akin to genius could he have been proved so excitingly right. This is collaborative art at its finest.

To be sure, collaboration is not always so exciting and so right. There are times when a screenwriter will feel that he is being walked all over and his work is being spat on—by everyone from the lighting technician to the makeup artist. And no matter how resilient he may try to be, he may still not be able to affect the outcome of a film in such a way as to retain the integrity of his original screenplay, and the film will suffer because of that. But as we said, those are the breaks of the game, and the sobering reality of the film industry is that, for better or worse, it is an unremittingly joint venture.

Even so, the worst incursion on a screenwriter's work should not ever let him lose sight of the dearest goal of his own craft—which is to be able to create a screenplay that is so clear and immediate and compelling, that given the very best of circumstances, it could get up off the page and film itself.

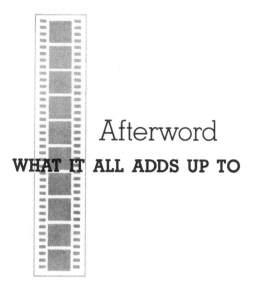

Afterword
WHAT IT ALL ADDS UP TO

Who knows how many films have already been made so far
in this twentieth century?

It's a pretty dizzying thought—who knows how anyone
would even go about trying to estimate such a thing?

We'd say there must be somewhere between 50,000
and 500,000 full-length feature films that have already been
shot since 1900. And we're talking here about legitimate
motion pictures, put out by bona fide studios or producers
or independent filmmakers, not just those fly-by-night
low-budget cheapo jobs that have been cranked out by the
tens of thousands to make a fast buck. And it's a little sad
to realize that of the total footage of all the legitimate
full-length feature films that have ever been made, a good
quantity of the earliest motion picture film stock would
be getting so grainy that it would be virtually unshowable
today.

So let's say we might have a total of a hundred billion
miles of footage of films that have already been made so far

in this twentieth century. But wait a minute—we're not taking into account all the millions and millions of miles of 8mm and 16mm home movies that have been made in almost all American families for generations. And then there are also the endless miles of newsreel film footage, as well as all the weekly serials that have ever been made, and all the military and medical and scientific filmage, to say nothing of the film that's used in some information storage retrieval systems, and all that film that's used in some security systems to record bank robberies. And of course we're not counting all the enormous footage of all the illicit hardcore porn films that have ever been shot in a burgeoning underground skin flick business that's been going on for decades. And if we add to this all the footage of all the TV tape film that's been shot in this century, including the recent exploding market for commercial videocassettes to be shown on home Betamax machines—well, now we're probably way up in the hundreds of trillions of feet of film.

It's probably safe to say that if all the film that's been shot so far in this twentieth century were laid end to end, it would stretch from one end of our solar system to the other end, and back again.

And that's a pretty staggering thought. But then, staggering numbers are what the film industry is all about.

There are hundreds of thousands of movie theatres out there in this country, and each week these theatres need new films to show to their audiences. And then these same films will be booked for overseas distribution to all the movie theatres around the world, and on turbojet airplanes, and onboard oceangoing luxury liners. And then these same films will be leased for endless showing on network and home box office and cable television.

The commodity market for new films is so obviously there, and filmmaking is so obviously an investment industry with a cost-profit factor built right into the medium, that one wonders when and how the business and artistic interests ever coincide, if indeed they ever do.

On the one hand, filmmaking has emerged as one of the

greatest money-making businesses of the twentieth century. Mogul studio empires, superstar acting careers, best-seller book sales to Hollywood, spinoff recording contracts, and a whole host of secondary professions have grown up around the film industry, everything from press agentry and stunt men to popcorn concessions and marquee letter manufacturers.

On the other hand, filmmaking has also emerged as the greatest of all twentieth century art forms. Nowhere can one create on such a grand scale—from Cecil B. DeMille's Biblical epics where Moses actually parts the Red Sea onscreen, to spectacular technical film effects like Stanley Kubrick's *2001: A Space Odyssey* where the dramatic setting is the entire universe. And nowhere can one create on such an intimate scale—from the intensely quiet moments of Ingmar Bergman's *Wild Strawberries* where an old man is trying to reclaim the emotional memory of his own childhood, to the self-conscious improvisational courtship of Diane Keaton and Woody Allen as they stand on a rooftop in *Annie Hall*.

In no other medium can one engage the eye and ear and mind and heart and imagination of an audience so totally, as in motion pictures.

Yet the conflict of books versus bucks is also so obviously there, and there will always be enormous pressures on anyone who is engaged in filmmaking to compromise his artistic interests for his business interests, and vice versa. And there's really not much more that one can say about this, except that it is a dilemma that goes with the territory.

Certainly no one feels this dilemma of art versus business more keenly than the professional screenwriter. On the one hand, he knows he is a writer for hire, a part of a larger collaborative enterprise which is strictly bound to its budget considerations, and everything the screenwriter ever writes will always be pitted against that remorseless economic standard. On the other hand, the screenwriter has his own artistic conscience to consider, and his sense that if he yields too much too easily, he may just compromise himself out of his livelihood, because he will lose touch with his own craft.

Clearly there is no resolution of this dilemma. All a screenwriter can ever do is be aware of the dilemma, and go on from there. Which is to say, he should keep on concentrating on his love for the ongoing process of screenwriting and filmmaking, because that is the reason he is involved in the work in the first place.

As one major screenwriting agent told us: "If people want to write, they will write—they cannot be discouraged from it."

Not only that—if a screenwriter really wants to write, he will also write as well as he possibly can. He will not allow himself to crank out a cynical hack job, or cook up a lot of lifeless lines to stick in the mouths of so many cliche cardboard characters. He will try to write, and he will endlessly rewrite until he has succeeded in recreating reality as he knows it.

One of our greatest writers put it this way:

Reality is an organic thing which the poetic imagination can represent, or suggest, in essence, only through transformation.[75]

Transformation of character is an awfully hard thing for anyone to get down on paper, but that's what the good screenwriter will always be going for. And that's why he will always do his damndest to write fluid and truthful lines for living and feeling human beings. Because, that's what excellent films are always all about, and that is what screenwriting is at its best.

CONTESTS

Following is a list of contests in the United States that are open to submission of filmscripts and screenplays. Guidelines and prizes and deadlines differ—some range from $200 to $500 to $1000, for short films or 120 minute full-length filmscripts. Screenwriters should send letter of inquiry asking for guidelines and deadlines, and enclose stamped, self-addressed envelope for each contest's guidelines and entry form.

Christopher Columbus Society
Screenplay Discovery Awards
433 North Camden Drive, Suite 600
Beverly Hills, CA 90210

NPT Screenplay Festival
New Professional Theatre
443 West 50th Street
New York, NY 10019

PEN Center USA West Literary Awards
672 South Lafayette Park Place, Suite 41
Los Angeles, CA 90057

Writers' Digest Writing Competition
1507 Dana Avenue
Cincinnati, OH 45207-1005

FELLOWSHIPS

Following is a list of foundation grants and fellowships that are available to screenwriters. The awards are almost always designated for the creation of new work, but the conditions and terms vary from one organization to another. One should send a letter of inquiry asking for guidelines and application forms, from each organization. Be sure to enclose a stamped, self-addressed envelope for each organization, with sufficient postage to cover a sometimes bulky packet of materials.

Artist Trust
1402 Third Avenue, Suite 404
Seattle, WA 98101-2118

Brody Arts Fund
California Community Foundation
606 South Olive Street, Suite 2400
Los Angeles, CA 90014-1526

Bush Artist Fellowships
The Bush Foundation
E-900 First National Bank Building
332 Minnesota Street
St. Paul, MN 55101

The Don And Gee Nicholl
Fellowships In Screenwriting
Academy of Motion Picture Arts & Sciences
8949 Wilshire Boulevard
Beverly Hills, CA 90211-1972

Fulbright Scholar Awards
Council For Internation Exchange of Scholar
3007 Tilden Street NW, Suite 5M, Box FEL
Washington, DC 20008-3009

National Endowment For The Arts
Media Arts Program
1100 Pennsylvania Avenue NW, Room 720
Washington, DC 20506

New York Foundation For The Arts
Artists' Fellowships
155 Avenue of the Americas, 14th Floor
New York, NY 10013-1507

Many Voices Multicultural Collaboration Grants
2301 Franklin Avenue East
Minneapolis, MN 55406-1099

The Walt Disney Studios Fellowship Program
500 South Buena Vista Street
Burbank, CA 91521-0880

Note: for emergency funds, screenwriters should contact The
Authors League Fund, 330 West 42nd Street, 29th Floor, New
York, NY 10036. For emergency grant or for interest-free loan,
apply to Carnegie Fund For Authors, 1 Old Country Road,
Suite 113, Carle Place, NY 11514. Try also PEN Writers Fund,
568 Broadway, New York, NY 10012.

AGENTS

Following is a list of agents in the United States who handle the work of screenwriters. One should never telephone or make any unannounced visits or send unsolicited filmscripts to these agents. Instead, one should send a letter of inquiry together with a brief resume and summary of one's work, and be sure to enclose a stamped, self-addressed envelope with the inquiry.

The Agency
1800 Avenue of the Stars, Suite 400
Los Angeles, CA 90067

Agency For The Performing Arts
888 Seventh Avenue, Suite 602
New York, NY 10106

Bertha Klausner International Literary Agency
71 Park Avenue
New York, NY 10016

Bret Adams Ltd.
448 West 44th Street
New York, NY 10036

Don Buchwald & Associates
10 East 44th Street
New York, NY 10017

Fifi Oscard Associates
24 West 40th Street, 17th Floor
New York, NY 10018

Helen Merrill
435 West 23rd Street, Suite 1A
New York, NY 10011

International Creative Management
40 West 57th Street
New York, NY 10019

The Kopaloff Company
1800 Avenue of the Stars, Suite 400
Los Angeles, CA 90067

The Roberts Company
10345 West Olympic Boulevard, Penthouse
Los Angeles, CA 90064

The Parness Agency
1424 4th Street, Suite 404
Santa Monica, CA 90401

Susan Schulman Literary Agency
454 West 44th Street
New York, NY 10036

William Morris Agency
1325 Avenue of the Americas
New York, NY 10019

Writers & Artists Agency
19 West 44th Street, Suite 1000
New York, NY 10036

COLONIES AND RESIDENCIES

Following is a list of colonies and retreats and residencies where screenwriters can pursue their work in congenial and uninterrupting environs. Application deadlines and terms of residency vary from place to place, so one should send a letter of inquiry with a stamped, self-addressed envelope, for guidelines of each organization.

Alden B. Dow Creativity Center
Northwood University
Midland, MI 48640-2398

Altos De Chavon
Parsons School of Design
2 West 13th Street, Room 707
New York, NY 10011

Headlands Center For The Arts
944 Fort Barry
Sausalito, CA 94965

Helene Wurlitzer Foundation of New Mexico
Box 545
Taos, NM 87571

The MacDowell Colony
100 High Street
Peterborough, NH 03458

The Millay Colony For The Arts
East Hill Road
Box 3
Austerlitz, NY 12017-0003

Shenandoah Playwright Residencies
Shenanarts
Rt. 5, Box 167-F
Staunton, VA 24401

The Tyrone Guthrie Center
Annaghmakerrig, Newbliss
County Monaghan, Ireland

Vermont Studio Center
Box 613NW
Johnson, VT 05656

Villa Montalvo Artist Residency Program
Box 158
Saratoga, CA 95071-0158

Virginia Center For The Creative Arts
Box VCCA, Mt. San Angelo
Sweet Briar, VA 24595

William Flanagan Memorial Creative Persons Center
Edward F. Albee Foundation
14 Harrison Street
New York, NY 10013

Yaddo
Box 395
Saratoga Springs, NY 12866-0395

ADDENDA TO CHAPTER ONE

Following is an updating of the list of American films 1925–1997, that appears on pages 14–18 of this book:

1925	*The Battleship Potemkin*
	Phantom of the Opera
1926	*The Scarlet Letter*
1927	*The Jazz Singer*
1934	*The Scarlet Pimpernel*
1939	*Gunga Din*
1940	*Abe Lincoln in Illinois*
	Our Town
1942	*The Pride of the Yankees*
1944	*Arsenic and Old Lace*

1946   *It's a Wonderful Life*

1952   *Julius Caesar*

1961   *West Side Story*

1962   *Long Day's Journey Into Night*

1968   *Rosemary's Baby*

1969   *Alice's Restaurant*
        Midnight Cowboy

1971   *A Clockwork Orange*

1973   *Mean Streets*
        Bang the Drum Slowly

1974   *Chinatown*

1975   *One Flew Over the Cuckoo's Nest*
        Nashville

1976   *Bound for Glory*
        Taxi Driver

1977   *Annie Hall*

1978   *The Deer Hunter*
        Coming Home

1979   *All That Jazz*
        Apocalypse Now

1980   *Raging Bull*
        Ordinary People
        Coalminer's Daughter

1981   *On Golden Pond*

1982   *Gandhi*

1985   *The Color Purple*
        Freud

1988   *The Unbearable Lightness of Being*

1989	*Born on the Fourth of July*
1991	*JFK*
1993	*Schindler's List* *The Piano*
1994	*Pulp Fiction* *Forest Gump*
1995	*Sense and Sensibility* *Leaving Las Vegas*
1996	*Independence Day* *Looking for Richard* *Nixon*
1997	*1001* *The Crucible* *The English Patient*

Following is an updating of the list of *foreign films* that appears on page 18 of this book:

ENGLAND	*Darling* *Petulia*
SPAIN	Luis Buñuel—*Los Olvidados* *Virdiana*
CHINA	Shang Yimou—*Raise The Red Lanterns* Chen Kaige—*Yellow Earth*
RUSSIA	Andrei Tarkovsky—*Andrei Roublev*
INDIA	Satyajit Ray—*Apur Sansar (The World Of Apu)*
FRANCE	Louis Maille—*Au Revoir Les Enfants*

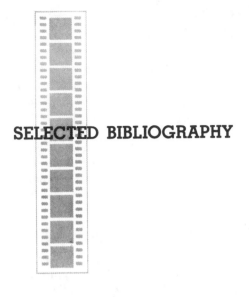

SELECTED BIBLIOGRAPHY

A word about books.

The early Vachel Lindsay book on *The Art of the Moving Picture,* originally issued in 1915, is not as generally known as it ought to be. Written twelve years before the advent of sound, this book is one of the very first attempts to treat film and filmmaking as a serious art form.

Then there are the two monumental classics about filmmaking—Sergei Eisenstein's two volumes on film theory, and James Agee's two volumes of film criticism. These books set down the technical and critical standards for film in our time, and no one who is interested in any aspect of filmmaking should be without them.

Then there is the more recent book by William Goldman, *Adventures in the Screen Trade,* which is well on its way to becoming a classic on the art of screenwriting. In addition to being a highly readable, amusing, and incisive book which ruthlessly exposes all the foibles of the film industry, Goldman's book also includes the complete original screenplay from his inimitable film, *Butch Cassidy and the Sundance Kid.*

In addition to these books, there are two other volumes which I drew on extensively—*Writers on Screenwriting*, and *Filmmaking: The Collaborative Art*. These two books are invaluable for their straightforward interviews and interesting documentation of the life and work of screenwriters and filmmakers who are actively engaged in the film industry.

All the other books on the following bibliography list are also worthwhile—some of them specialize in marketing techniques, some of them are concerned with film theory, and some of them concentrate on individual film achievements of particular artists. I should especially mention Kenneth MacGowan's fine book, *Behind the Screen: The History and Techniques of the Motion Picture*.

There are a couple of screenwriting textbooks on the list also—not bad books, but obviously I felt there was a need for a more comprehensive text that would incorporate the history of film, film theory, and the actual practice of filmmaking, together with guidelines on agentry and marketing of screenplays, with sections devoted to film treatments and proper screenplay format. Which is why I set about writing this book in the first place.

I should say that I'm responsible for the translations of the Verlaine poem in Chapter Three, and for the translations of Japanese haiku that appear in Chapter Five.

WILLIAM PACKARD

Bibliography

ON THE TECHNIQUES OF
SCREENWRITING AND FILMMAKING

James Agee, *Agee on Film*—Volumes One and Two,
  Wideview / Perigee Book, Putnam (1958).
Rudolf Arnheim, *Film as Art*,
  University of California Press (1957).
Richard Barsaw, *Nonfiction Film Theory and Criticism*,
  Dutton (1976).
Keith Burr/Joseph Gillis, *The Screenwriters Guide:
  The Handbook for Film and Television Sales*,
  Zoetrope (1982).
Donald Chase, *Filmmaking: The Collaborative Art*,
  Little, Brown & Company (1975).
Sergei Eisenstein, *Film Form/Film Sense
  Essays on Film Theory*, Harvest Book, Harcourt Brace & World (1949).
Syd Field, *Screenplay: The Foundations of Screenwriting*,
  Delacorte Press (1979).
William Goldman, *Adventures in the Screen Trade*,
  Warner Books (1983).
Lewis Jacobs, *The Movies*,
  Noonday Press, Farrar Straus Girous (1960).
Stanley Kaufman, *A World on Film*,
  Delta (1958).
Arthur Knight, *The Liveliest Art*,
  Mentor/New American Library (1957).

Richard F. Leavitt, *The World of Tennessee Williams,*
    W. H. Allen, London (1978).
Carl Linder, *Filmmaking: A Practical Guide,*
    Spectrum/Prentice-Hall (1976).
Vachel Lindsay, *The Art of the Moving Picture,*
    Liveright, (1915, 1970).
Kenneth MacGowan, *Behind the Screen The History and Techniques of the Motion Picture,*
    Delta/Dell (1965).
Joseph McBride, *Film Makers on Film Making,*
    Houghton-Miflin Co. (1983).
Paul Michael, *The Academy Awards: A Pictorial History,*
    Bonanza Books (1964).
Laurence Olivier, *Confessions of an Actor,*
    Penguin (1982).
Gerald Pratley, *The Cinema of Otto Preminger,*
    Castle Books (1971).
Otto Preminger, *Preminger: An Autobiography,*
    Doubleday (1977).
Daniel Talbot, *Film, an Anthology,*
    University of California Press (1966).
Tony Thomas, *The Films of Marlon Brando,*
    Citadel Press (1973).
Coles Trapnell, *Teleplay: An Introduction to Television Writing,*
    Hawthorne Books (1966).
Alexander Walker, *Stanley Kubrick Directs,*
    Harcourt, Brace, Jovanovich (1971).
Tennessee Williams, *Memoirs*
    Doubleday (1972).
Word into Image: Writers on Screenwriting,
    American Film Foundation (1981).
Maurice Yacowar, *Tennessee Williams and Film,*
    Frederick Ungar (1977).

NOTES

1. D. H. Lawrence, *The Theatre*.
2. Rudolph Arnheim, *Film as Art*.
3. Tennessee Williams, *The Glass Menagerie*.
4. James Agee, *Agee on Film*, 1.
5. Otto Preminger, *Preminger: An Autobiography*, Doubleday (1977).
6. Charlie Chaplin, "How I Made My Success," *Theatre Magazine*, New York (September, 1915).
7. Joan Fontaine, interview with William Packard (1984).
8. Tennessee Williams, *Memoirs*, Doubleday (1971).
9. Otto Preminger, *Preminger: An Autobiography*, Doubleday (1977).
10. Sergei Eisenstein, *The Film Sense*.
11. Laurence Olivier, *Confessions of an Actor*.
12. Orson Welles, *The New Statesman* (May 24, 1958.)
13. Mary Harden, The Bret Adams Agency, interview with William Packard (1984).
14. Kenneth MacGowan, *Behind the Screen*.
15. Alexander Walker, *Stanley Kubrick Directs*.
16. William Goldman, *Writers on Screenwriting*.
17. James Agee, "Agee on Film," *The Nation* (March 10, 1945).
18. Ingmar Bergman, "Each Film is My Last," *Tulane Drama Review*, T 33 (Fall 1966).
19. George Bernard Shaw, *Metropolitan Magazine*, cited in Lindsay, *The Art of the Moving Picture*.
20. Erwin Panofsky, "Style and Medium in the Motion Pictures," *Film: An Anthology*, ed., Daniel Talbot.
21. Gerald Pratley, *The Cinema of Otto Preminger*, Castle Books (1971).
22. Otto Preminger, *Preminger: An Autobiography*, Doubleday (1977).
23. Maurice Tacowar, *Tennessee Williams and Film*.
24. Nunnally Johnson, *Filmmaking: The Collaborative Art*.
25. *Ibid*.
26. Ray Bradbury, *Filmmaking: The Collaborative Art*.
27. William Goldman, *Word into Image: Writers on Screenwriting*.
28. Neil Simon, *Writers on Screenwriting*.

29. Alvin Sargent, *Filmmaking: The Collaborative Art*.
30. Merian Cooper, *Filmmaking: The Collaborative Art*.
31. William Goldman, *Writers on Screenwriting*.
32. Carl Foreman, *Writers on Screenwriting*.
33. Neil Simon, *Writers on Screenwriting*.
34. *Ibid*.
35. Alexander Walker, *Stanley Kubrick Directs* (1971).
36. Ingmar Bergman, *Filmmakers on Filmmaking*.
37. Leo Connellan, interview with William Packard (1984).
38. Sigmund Freud, *The Interpretation of Dreams* (1900).
39. Carl Foreman, *Writers on Screenwriting*.
40. William Goldman, *Adventures in the Screen Trade*.
41. Carl Foreman, *Writers on Screenwriting*.
42. Rosanne Ehrlich, Paramount Pictures, interview with William Packard (1984).
43. Venable Herndon, interview with William Packard (1985).
44. Eleanor Perry, *Writers on Screenwriting*.
45. Rosanne Ehrlich, interview with William Packard (1984).
46. Studio summary of *Giant*; from Venable Herndon, *James Dean: A Short Life*, Doubleday (1974).
47. Venable Herndon, Screenplay Treatment for *First Father*.
48. Paul Mazursky, *Writers on Screenwriting*.
49. William Goldman, *Writers on Screenwriting*.
50. Tennessee Williams, Notes to *One Arm Stopped Rocking*, New Directions (1984).
51. Rosanne Ehrlich, Paramount Pictures, interview with William Packard (1984).
52. *Alice's Restaurant*, copyright @ 1969, Florio Corporation; 1970, Arthur Penn; 1970, Doubleday.
53. William Goldman, *Adventures in the Screen Trade*, Warner Books (1983).
54. *Butch Cassidy and the Sundance Kid*, copyright @ 1969 by William Goldman.
55. Tennessee Williams, *One Arm Stopped Rocking and Other Plays*, New Directions (1984).
56. Bret Adams, interview with William Packard (1984).
57. *Ibid*.
58. Rosanne Ehrlich, Paramount Pictures, interview with William Packard (1984).
59. Otto Preminger, *Preminger: An Autobiography*, Doubleday (1977).
60. Eleanor Perry, *Writers on Screenwriting*.
61. Writers Guild of America, interview with William Packard (1984).
62. Joan Fontaine, interview with William Packard (1984).
63. Venable Herndon, interview with William Packard (1984).

64. Venable Herndon, interview with William Packard (1984).
65. Rosanne Ehrlich, Paramount Pictures, interview with William Packard (1984).
66. Bret Adams, interview with William Packard (1984).
67. Robert Towne, *Writers on Screenwriting*.
68. Joan Fontaine, interview with William Packard (1984).
69. Writers Guild of America, interview with William Packard (1984).
70. Venable Herndon, *James Dean: A Short Life*, Doubleday (1974).
71. Billy Wilder, *Filmmakers on Filmmaking*.
72. Budd Schulberg, *Filmmaking: The Collaborative Art*.
73. *Ibid.*
74. James Wong Howe, *Filmmakers on Filmmaking*.
75. Tennessee Williams, production notes for *The Glass Menagerie*.

INDEX

191